PT
2685   BEST, O F
.E5   PETER WEISS
Z5813

NORTHAMPTON COMMUNITY
DISCARDED
COLLEGE LIBRARY

NORTHAMPTON COUNTY AREA
Learning Resources Center
Bethlehem, Pa. 18017
COMMUNITY COLLEGE

PETER WEISS

In the same series:

MODERN LITERATURE MONOGRAPHS

GENERAL EDITOR: Lina Mainiero

PETER WEISS

Otto F. Best

Translated by Ursule Molinaro

NORTHAMPTON COUNTY AREA
Learning Resources Center
Bethlehem, Pa. 18017
COMMUNITY COLLEGE

FREDERICK UNGAR PUBLISHING CO.
NEW YORK

Translated from the German
Peter Weiss by Otto F. Best
originally published by Francke Verlag, Bern
with revisions and additions by the author

Copyright © 1976 by Frederick Ungar Publishing Co., Inc.
Printed in the United States of America
Designed by Anita Duncan

Library of Congress Cataloging in Publication Data

Best, Otto F   1929-
  Peter Weiss.

  (Modern literature monographs)
  Bibliography: p.
  Includes index.
    1.   Weiss, Peter, 1916-   —Criticism and interpre-
tation.
PT2685.E5Z5813   832'.9'14   75-10104
ISBN 0-8044-2038-6

Contents

Chronology

1962	*Gespräch der drei Gehenden.* Book publication in 1963. Begins work on *Marat/Sade.*
1962–63	*Nacht mit Gästen.* World première 1963.
1963	First and second version of *Marat/Sade is* completed. Awarded the Charles Veillon Prize for *Fluchtpunkt.* Begins work on *Mockinpott,* which is completed and first produced in 1968.
1964	April 29. World première of *Marat/Sade* at the Schiller-Theater, Berlin. Early summer. Spectator at the Auschwitz trial in Frankfurt. *Die Ermittlung.* World première in 1965.
1965	Awarded the Lessing Prize by the city of Hamburg, and the literary prize of the Swedish workers' education movement.
1966	Awarded the Heinrich Mann Prize of the Deutsche Akademie der Künste. *Gesang vom Lusitanischen Popanz.* World première in 1967.
1966–68	*Viet Nam Diskurs.* World première in 1968.
1967	Travels to Cuba.
1968	Travels to North Vietnam. Publication of *Viet Nam Notizen.* Publication of "Das Material und die Modelle." *Rapporte* (essays).
1968–69	*Trotzki im Exil.* World première and publication in 1970.
1971	*Rapporte 2* *Hölderlin* (play)
1972	*Rekonvaleszenz* (diary) *Das Duell* (narration)

A Note on Usage

Throughout this edition, Weiss's works are referred to by
their English title except on first occurrence, when the
English title (in parentheses) is preceded by the German
title. In the case of long titles, the customary short forms
are used throughout except on first occurrence in the
chapter discussing the work in question. Wherever a
published translation of a work exists, this has been
indicated by preceding the English title in parentheses by
"tr." and all available English translations have been included in the bibliography at the end of this volume.
Where an English translation exists, quotations have been
taken from the translation. A few significant changes
between originals and translations have been indicated
in footnotes.

Introduction

"My own evolution toward Marxism went through many stages, from surrealist experimentation, from periods of doubt, skepticism, and belief in the most absurd concepts, to radical political commitment." Written in 1967, this sentence characterizes Peter Weiss's journey from ego-centric, almost autistic inner contemplation to political action within the collective, from existentialist drama to Marxist world theater.

Coming to terms with the established values that had shaped his early life led him through a state where he lived without values and eventually to the adoption of new values. The dialogue between Marat and Sade mirrors this gradual development. Sade's statement that it is not possible to find truths other than "the changeable truths of one's own experience" loses its previous validity and becomes subject to doubt.

While striving for the freedom of subjective experience and formal experimentation, the writer's aesthetic and political development also struggled toward total political freedom. The question is whether psychoanalysis can be combined with politics, the individual with the collective, and aesthetics with action. Does fighting for one automatically eliminate the other, as the political-philosophical discussion between Sade and Marat claims? What is the price of release from lostness, of "meaningful" acceptance into the collective?

The works of Peter Weiss, founded on self-portrayal

1

and self-analysis, form a single oeuvre. A writer's confession, it becomes self-contained through the logical
reworking of specific themes, subjects, and forms that can
be traced back to the author's early beginnings. His
private life, biography, and writing are therefore inter-
twined to an almost extreme degree.

It would be a mistake to speak of a contradiction
between "early" and "later" Weiss. His writings before
Marat/Sade must be considered the precondition for his
subsequent work, and his desire for an "unambiguous
and precise" world is understandable in the light of his
anguish and confusion. The words he dedicated to Strindberg apply equally well to him: "He dared to express his
inner conflict, he dared to reveal himself with all his
contradictions." But the radical difference between the
influential Swedish writer and Peter Weiss is that Strindberg had the ability to retreat from his achievements, to
revise himself. Peter Weiss lacks this skill. With stubborn
consistency he took the road that finally led to a spiritual
no-man's land. The change from private to political
problems, the transition from surrealist grotesques to
so-called political documentary theater occurred in a process that ultimately enthroned the author once more as
the glorifier of a higher order.

The development from *Der Turm* (tr. *The Tower*) to
Viet Nam Diskurs (tr. *Discourse on Viet Nam*), and even
to *Trotski im Exil* (tr. *Trotsky in Exile*), follows a pattern that may most closely be defined as dualism—the
antitheses of passive-active, son-father, violation-libera-
tion, victim-executioner, individualist-revolutionary, op-
pressor-oppressed, exploited-exploiter. The opposing
concepts tend to link personal and subjective concerns to
a larger universal context and create an electric field
controlled by elements of violence and obsession.

From the fantastic world of silent menace in *Der
Schatten des Körpers des Kutschers* (tr. *The Shadow of
the Coachman's Body*) the road leads past analysis and
denunciation of the forces that cause torture, disgust,

isolation, and the need for revolution, by way of *Marat/Sade*, to the confrontation of victim and executioner in *Die Ermittlung* (tr. *The Investigation*) and *Discourse on Viet Nam*, which interpreted the tension ideologically and incorporates it in a larger, less ambiguous dualism. Instead of the psychological, biographically rooted question about the possible identity of lamb and wolf, which has become the dominating question of our century, these works raise the political themes of oppression as a phenomenon caused by a social system and of resistance to oppression. Chronologically, Peter Weiss's work clearly reflects a process in which conflicting theses press for solution and resolution.

Freedom Through Bondage:
The Tower

Peter Weiss was twenty-four when his reputation was established in Germany almost overnight by his short novel *The Shadow of the Coachman's Body*. His descriptive technique was considered an innovation and began to set a trend.

Born in Nowawes, near Berlin, on November 8, 1916, Weiss grew up in Bremen and Berlin. At the age of eighteen, he emigrated to London with his parents. Two years later, in 1936, the first exhibition of his paintings and experimental films was held in London. From 1936 to 1938 he studied at the art academy in Prague. Then he followed his parents to Sweden, where, in 1940, he was given a second exhibition of paintings and experimental films. His first book, a collection of prose poems called *Fran ö till ö* (From Island to Island), was published in Sweden in 1946. His play *Der Turm* (tr. *The Tower*), though written in 1948, was not performed in Germany until 1962.

It is an undeniable fact that German postwar theater owes to Peter Weiss one of its best plays, *Die Verfolgung und Ermordung Jean Paul Marats* (tr. *The Persecution and Assassination of Jean-Paul Marat*)—generally known merely as *Marat/Sade*—and that the "micronovel" *The Shadow* was a crucial stimulus to the renewal and continued development of epic structure in German literature. Both works follow a pattern of experience and structure that goes back to *The Tower*.

This one-act play, written for radio performance, has mistakenly been dismissed as a youthful folly by the author of *Marat/Sade*. When *The Tower* was performed in 1948 in an experimental theater in Stockholm, it received rather unfavorable reviews and was not published in Germany for many years. Though it is Peter Weiss's earliest preserved theatrical writing, with all the obvious faults of a first work, it is nevertheless worth our consideration and deserves to introduce a study of the author for reasons besides chronology.

Though the title is reminiscent of Calderón, Hofmannsthal, and W. B. Yeats, Weiss does not seem to intend any reference or allusion. There is no evidence of a connection beyond the obvious use of the tower symbol. The subject of the play is awareness of captivity and desire for liberation, for release from a community ruled by values of the past, for self-fulfillment that leads to freedom within the personal identity. It is a common theme in twentieth-century literature.

The hero, Pablo, returns to the tower, a symbolical locality, where, many years before, he had lived as part of a circus community. Though he had broken away to live his own life, escape did not free him from the world of the tower within. His reason for returning to the restrictive circle of the enclosure is the realization that he must come to terms with it, that he cannot simply run away. The goal must not be flight but the conquest and assimilation of his own past. It must be a liberation achieved not by escapist forgetfulness, but by a clarifying confrontation, even at the risk of a final defeat.

Pablo's various roles in the circus of the tower correspond to the phases of his struggle. He started out doing a balancing act and "switched to a one-man hanging act," toying with death. His idea of freedom is therefore defined negatively, since he can perceive it only as a diminution of the rope's strangulating pressure. Authoritarian upbringing, destroying the personality, equivalent to animal training, is the obvious purpose of the first circus act; the answer to it, playing with death and suicide, is contained in the second. The third stunt, the reason for his return to his circus "family," is to bring him liberation. He will give a performance as an escape artist and free himself to experience life and his own personality. "I'm only here now in order to break out!"

Pablo enters the tower as an odyssean Nemo, as "Niente," a nothing, in order to earn his own name. The author uses the age-old concept that a person's identity is expressed in his name. Pable had left Carlo, his alter ego, in the prison. Carlo symbolizes Pablo's continued existence as a prisoner of the tower. Instead of Pablo's action, Carlo looks for escape and substitution in pantomime—in art, in aestheticism.

The magician is the crucial figure in the "fortress" of the tower, which is filled with echo effects and with the ticking of clocks to indicate uniformity, eternal sameness. He embodies all that "craves death." "Without any apparent occupation, he is the strongest force in the tower." He embodies death, an ever-present alternative to captivity. Enduring time as a captive, fleeing from time as a suicide, or acting against time as a revolutionary—these are the existential options Weiss discusses and portrays more or less directly in his work.

The inside of the tower remains completely unchanged, confirming a characteristic of Weiss's early works—that the solitary individual can separate himself from his environment, that he can withdraw into himself, change, and find himself through change, but that he must accept as a given the social structure into which he was born and in which he grew up. A dream sequence, which takes place on a second plane of this play, which is itself dreamlike with its twilight world of inner images, once more invokes the atmosphere of tyrannical family life that Pablo had left behind by fleeing. It consists of order, duty, reference to tradition, the demand for discipline, submission, adjustment.

The desire to die prompted by despair and the desire

to live prompted by curiosity, complementary forces, stand juxtaposed. Pablo dares to escape only with the circus lion, the symbol of boundless though bound life. The feeling of resignation expressed as a desire for death is replaced by the venture with life. This change is exemplified by the lion's dying at the very moment Pablo attains freedom, although only external freedom. In the same manner Carlo subsequently disappears at the very moment Pablo succeeds in shedding his chains.

As the lion symbolizes life and the tower represents the absence of freedom, so Nelly stands for love—a demanding kind of love, which itself creates an aspect of the prison. This fact explains why Pablo first withholds himself from Nelly, the "specter of love," but spends "every night" with her after her death, in an open love that is free of real bonds, while Carlo, his alter ego, "was with her every night" and thus is doubly bound. Left behind in the tower, where omnipotent tradition creates loneliness and alienation instead of solidarity, Carlo lives on after Pablo's flight with his "most genuine, deeply experienced feelings" as a substitute for freedom and action. The dwarf takes over the role of the lion. His is a crippled life, representing one possibility for Carlo's— and consequently for Pablo's—existence. In his person the life force has become so harmless, so toothless and impervious to external temptations that he is allowed to leave the tower at any time.

Finally Pablo gives the gala performance that brought him back to the tower. In public view the escape artist Niente is tied with ropes by the dwarf and the magician, the "trusty assistants" of the circus. While Pablo struggles to extricate himself, various scenes, performed during his exertions, reflect the following alternatives to Pablo's liberation. Carlo dances emotions—love, fear, humility, devotion. All of these are what Nietzsche would call slave virtues. The shadow duelist fights a "duel with himself" and triumphs over himself. The lion tamer offers the most tangible alternatives with her act, which

alludes to ruling and pedagogic principles that have pre-
vailed in Europe for thousands of years. These acts are
interrupted at times by the magician who describes Pablo's
struggle in the style of a sports broadcaster.

Pablo succeeds in extricating himself from his
bonds, gaining freedom and, with it, a past. There is no
clearer way to demonstrate liberation as birth. It could
not be illustrated more clearly. "The rope dangles down
from him now like an umbilical cord," notes a voice,
"very slowly, matter-of-factly, cool." The world of the
tower has "drowned." There is "silence." The goal has
been reached. Nevertheless, "you have to be free even
beforehand, before you even start. The actual breaking
loose becomes a mere matter of confirmation then," the
play states at the outset. It opens Pablo's "essence" to
receive life, existence, and it adds "time" to "being."
Echoes of existentialist thought abound.

The Tower is a parable, a variant on the story of
the prodigal son. By his return, Pablo, the oppressed,
initialed the round dance of figures which represent the
self's process of becoming according to its own ground
plan and illustrate the tensions between father and son,
ruler and populace, masters and colonials, and so on. This
dynamic is one of the basic problems with which Peter
Weiss deals repeatedly by extending it to an ever wider
periphery.

The prodigal son returns, not to seek forgiveness
and mercy but to claim his rights. His heritage consists
not of material goods but of the inalienable right to realize
his freedom in opposition to the massive brunt of the
material world and of the metaphysical determining
factors in world and society, the smallest unit of which is
the "family."

In the tower Pablo was a means to an end. Training
had reduced him to an "object," to be exploited. According to Kant, this corresponds to a negation of human
dignity. Rebellion, then, becomes the act of creative sub-
jectivity against the leveling powers of matter, tradition,

and society. Rebellion becomes the act of self-creation. Sartre has called man the being who creates himself, and he considers this the first existentialist principle. In other words, man is merely as he conceives himself. The world of the tower is the world of essence that precedes existence. The goal of Pablo's rebellion is the melding of essence with existence, since this process will change him from an "object" into a "person," into a subject.

Peter Weiss has dealt with this conflict in human life—a conflict that is not only unresolved but ultimately unresolvable, this groping for the road toward "a life of one's own," up to the moment when the seeker is "expelled into absolute freedom." He described it once again in his records of captivity and eventual release, his confessional works *Abschied von den Eltern* (tr. *Leavetaking*) and *Fluchtpunkt* (tr. *Vanishing Point*).

Vanishing Point contains a reference to Jean-Paul Sartre, the most influential proponent of French existentialism. Weiss was probably familiar with Sartre's thought when he wrote *The Tower* for radio and the stage. If we interpret the "fortress" of the tower as the "in-itself" of the world—rigid, "unchangeable," without a past, in which the clock strikes without telling time because "the whole tower is filled with time," "unending," "ever-present," and as the "world of other people" who are Sartre's "hell" as well—then the "for-itself" of the I Pablo tries to achieve stands in a relationship of tension to the tower's hermetic enclosure. Pablo's "for-itself" as openness, as a projection of a personal existence extending "outward," into the future, demands the "annihilation" of his own (enforced) past, which is at the same time the (eternal) present within the tower.

Fear had determined his earlier life. Fear must make man "aware of his freedom," Sartre has written, fear being "freedom's way of being aware of Being." "I only 'trusted' you because I was so frightened of you," Pablo tells the magician who embodies "the death addiction," the threat of the rigidity of nothingness. "I was terrorized

by your staring, stark white face!" White and immobility
are the attributes of death. Fear, prompted by the experience of vulnerability, impotence, and instability,
concretized as terror, recalls the fear of Kierkegaard,
Heidegger, and Sartre.

Only by completely putting himself into the hands of
the threatening element, the alien, death-inducing element, by letting himself be bound and thus risking the
leap into total bondage, like Sartre's Orestes, does Pablo
create the space for his freedom. By letting himself be
roped, he opposes death and terror-inducing nothingness
with existence-inducing action.

"Hell is other people," says Sartre. Dependence on
other people is considered the primal misfortune of
humanity. For one person's exercise of freedom negates
the freedom of the other. The figures of the magician and
the dwarf represent this complementary opposition. The
magician embodies the socially binding forces of religion
and myth, society's stereotypes of thought and action,
while the dwarf is its product, representative of a controlled, adapted world. On the other hand, total freedom
leads to chaos, since the liberating act of revolution
nullifies itself in anarchy, in which everybody "wants a
taste of blood" (*Marat/Sade*). In *Marat/Sade* Peter
Weiss exposed this contradiction on stage.

According to Sartre, the hellish nature of this world
leads to two basic types of behavior: masochism, in the
form of (passionate) submission to the existence of others
(as the character of Carlo), and sadism, in the form of
(passionate) negation and domination of the others (the
director, the manageress, and most of all the magician).
The relationship of oppressed and oppressor fuses both
types of conduct into a diabolical unity.

Sartre mentions still a third possibility—the realization of universal lawmaking, of action that "creates the
man we want to be" and at the same time "an image of
man as we think he should be." This "new man" may be
the *homme révolté* in Pablo's sense; alternately he may

be the new socialist man, after whose appearance sadistic
and masochistic obsessions will continue to exist exclusively in the (capitalist) inferno of a world that has been
split in two.

The metaphor of the tower occurs in the opening and
closing lines of the play of that name. Peter Weiss's play
about the (infernal) suffering of the German poet
Hölderlin, written almost twenty-five years later, begins
and ends with an allusion to the tower in which Hölderlin
spent the last days of his life. History takes the place of
autobiography.

Peter Weiss's first published play owes much to
Strindberg's subjective analytical dramatic technique
focused on the self, which is rooted in interior rumination
and personal experience, in the "development of one's
own soul," since, according to Strindberg, it is possible
"to know only one life, one's own." Peter Weiss's second
play strives for a new impetus and takes up where Yvan
Goll left off. Both Strindberg and Goll were important for
expressionism, so that a tradition is already in the
making; it did not remain without influence on Weiss.

Expressionism views the father as the defender of the
existing order. He controls the son. It is because of him
that the middle-class home has become a fortress. He, the
tyrant, the symbol of hated pressure, is the target of
radical negation. Kafka's *Letter to My Father* (1919)
bears witness to this tension and opposition. Since it is
the father who establishes and represents the norms, since
he decides what is "productive," liberation of the self
and self-assertion must lead to a feeling of futility. The
consequence is a sense of guilt. Thus the motifs of conflict between the generations, artistic problems, the sense
of guilt are conditional on each other. Kafka knew no
way to break out. For Peter Weiss, rebellion leads to
the idea of revolution and ultimately to worldwide revolution. In the autobiographical *Leavetaking* and *Vanishing
Point* he gives an undisguised report of these problems.

To keep to strict chronology, another play, *Die*

Versicherung (*The Insurance Policy*), written in 1952, should be discussed next. In this grotesque Peter Weiss turns from the subjective dramatic method to deal with contemporary society, which he ridicules with harsh, bitter irony. Before turning to plays that preceded *Marat/ Sade*, however, we will focus on the two autobiographical works which present paradigms and clarifications of the problems of development and liberation already dealt with in *The Tower*.

Self-Analysis and Confession: *Leavetaking* and *Vanishing Point*

Abschied von den Eltern (tr. *Leavetaking*) and *Fluchtpunkt* (tr. *Vanishing Point*) are important contributions to the genre of confessional literature. Both works are marked by the attempt to reconstruct the past in its entirety, to create an "objective" image of childhood, adolescence, and early adulthood. In the course of the confession events that are in the narrator's past take on shape and form in the present.

In each work a narrator gives an account of the contradictory nature which he discovers within himself and which he considers typical of his world and of his time. The authenticity of subjective frankness characterizes both works. The intensity of experience is controlled by a clear prose style that adheres to the exigencies of strict classical tradition. If *Leavetaking* is closer to the tradition of Rousseau's *Confessions* in its combination of self-analysis and truth-telling, *Vanishing Point* follows the pattern of the formative novel and especially of the novel of development, which delineate the confrontation with the formative environment from a negative angle. In the end the prodigal son's sole possessions are freedom and language.

The narrative *Leavetaking*, written in the period 1960–1961, is a record of psychological captivity. Its points of departure are the death of the narrator's father during a business trip to Belgium, the son's return home with the urn, and the definitive destruction of the family, which had begun with his sister's death in Berlin. Impulses from the narrator's "earliest life" surface in the act of leavetaking. Once again he lives through "the helplessness, the feeling of having been handed over and the blind rebellion" of those days, when strangers' hands "tamed, kneaded, and did violence" to his being.

Even as a child he suffers from the contrast between the "stuffiness," "the confinement" of the house—the same sensation Weiss attempted to express by the image of the tower in his first play—and the "world outside," in which he sees a kingdom belonging to him alone. When the narrator describes the child's favorite hiding places, he speaks not of refuge, but of "exile," a place of banishment. This image may be considered a key concept.

The awareness of being excluded, different, forced into a mold shaped by strangers, of which his name is a part, impels him to ignore his name, to pretend that he is deaf. Naming becomes the first outrage. In *The Tower* Pablo relinquishes his name, calls himself Niente, and struggles to earn his own name by self-liberation.

The first schoolday increases the narrator's fear to the point of panic, which takes on reality in images of obsession. The world becomes "enchanted"; buildings are "fortresslike"; men appear with "knives." The classroom becomes a torture chamber; nights are filled with "inconceivables," with "horror." "Every night," the narrator says, "I died, strangled, suffocated." The daytime world, with its shocks and its pain, continues in nightmares and nocturnal excursions. But a new experience is added to the misery and the pain: desire. "This alloy of pain and pleasure set its stamp on the fantasies of my dissipations." The hero "savored all the sorrows of humiliation."

The titles of the books that "pierce the heart" of the adolescent reflect the stage and level of development of body and mind. *"The Possessed, The Insulted and the Injured, The House of the Dead, The Devil's Elixir, Black Flags, Inferno*—these were the titles that suddenly

flared up in front of me and lit up something within me."
Fear and a feeling of menace become tangible and the
stuff that shapes one's fate when he listens to a speech
that sounded like "an incoherent screaming from hell."
His experience of Hitler's voice marks a crucial change:
the boy learns that his father is a Jew. The news comes
as a "confirmation" of something he had long suspected.
He begins to understand his past. It becomes clear why
he has been persecuted, jeered at, stoned. The narrator
instantly feels "entirely on the side of the underdog and
the outcast"; he comprehends his lostness, his rootlessness.

His experience and the subsequent recognition—
which suddenly furnishes an explanation, a reason for
suffering that had previously been incomprehensible—
allow him to define his own position. Culminating in the
public dialogue between Marat and Sade—a clarifying
conversation between the author and himself—this awareness becomes the existential reason for writing.

When his favorite sister is run over by a car, shortly
before the family's emigration to England, the dissolution
of the family begins, and the author paints his first large
picture. "Three figures in white costumes, doctors or
judges, loomed out of the black background, their faces
were bowed in an oppressive severity, their lowered
glances refused all mercy."

He paints what he feels, in order to come to terms
with it. Art is used as a means of successfully objectifying personal problems.

In London the narrator becomes an unpaid clerk in
a department store. He feels that he has been "banished."
This stint is followed by many months in his father's
office. He senses accusations, estrangement, lack of com-
prehension.

Jacques brings a new dimension into his life. "By
evoking my pictures for Jacques I was reminded that I
possessed another life, a different life from my life between
sample catalogues and rolls of material." In his conversations with Jacques the hero suddenly loses all fear of life.

"Jacques had already fought himself free, he had already conquered his consuming freedom. He had exposed himself to unprotectedness and wounds. In his life there was the wildness and unruliness that I had sought, but also the hunger and the distress." This friendship causes serious disagreements with his parents, the "totem poles of father and mother." The son finds himself faced with the alternatives of severing all bonds with his old life or reverting to his former self. He takes leave of his alter ego, the figure that had in many respects been "a wish image," and drops back into the old captivity, into lostness and "instability."

In Hermann Hesse's *Steppenwolf* the young man finds a description of his situation, "the situation of the bourgeois who wants to become a revolutionary but is crippled by the weight of established convention."

However, he also realizes that this book has trapped him "in a romantic no man's land, in self-pity." "I could have used to advantage a harder and more cruel voice, one which would have torn the veil from my eyes and made me rise and shine."

Meanwhile the family has moved to Czechoslovakia, where his father had been assigned the management of a textile factory. The narrator enrolls in the art academy in Prague—his parents have granted him a trial year. During his first night in the city he hears his "name" called as he sleeps, the name he had denied, which had been violently forced upon him, like Pablo's in *The Tower*.

He lives in Prague for a year. Family tyranny is replaced by self-tyranny. He feels guilty, cursed, incapable of commitment; in his sexual impotence he tends toward sadism because "the core of life" seems unattainable. The experiment in freedom and independence is a failure. He is tormented by thoughts of suicide. Gradually he comes to the realization that only one solution remains; to return to the house of his parents like a prodigal son who is "offered the grace" of shelter.

In the meantime the family has moved on to
Sweden. There the narrator goes to work in his father's
factory. He is a "foreign body," living in the "vacuum
between the world of my parents and the world of the
workmen." He feels his return as a "defeat." Emigration
now seems to him like the confirmation of the "not-
belonging" he has been experiencing since earliest childhood. The following two years are "a period of waiting,
a period of sleep-walking." When it is over, at the end
of the book, the "break-up" begins "with a violent
blow."

To sum up, it may be said that if the child and the
adolescent found the experience of menace and suffering
explained by his Jewish origin, the young man found in
his emigration the reason for his not-belonging, which
implied his failure. The child's fears suddenly appear in
a worldwide political context. A dream experience marks
the beginning of the break. The appearance of a "man in
a hunter's outfit" symbolizes the awakening, the abandonment of passivity, the end of weakness and discouragement; the hero is on the road toward a life of his own.
The hunted becomes the hunter, stalking himself. He is
filled with the vital force that will give his outcast state
a proper core. Henry Miller takes the place of Kafka,
as the author puts it in *Vanishing Point*.

Written in the period 1960–1961, *Vanishing Point*
is a more expansive novel. The searchlight of memory
has a wider beam, illuminating a number of secondary
experiences.

While *Leavetaking* was centered on the confrontation
with the family, with its conventions and restrictions, the
narrator of *Vanishing Point* begins to question a world
that has always been divided into antitheses, into the two
camps of victim and executioner, the weak and the strong,
the oppressed and the oppressor. At particular times
political constellations may reflect these oppositions. A
feeling of internal schism is added to the sensation of
lostness. The narrator embodies the notion that he con-

tains within himself the dual possibility of victim and executioner.

In *Leavetaking* the hero briefly experienced the good fortune of admission to the ranks of the strong, although he knows that he belongs to the weak. *Vanishing Point* refers back to this event when the narrator joins "the party of the stronger" whom he "outdid in cruelty" "out of thankfulness at being spared." He adds, "The only thing I saw clearly was that I could be on the side of the persecutor and hangman. I had it in me to take part in an execution."

In almost suicidal fashion, commanding respect and gratitude, Peter Weiss touches on one of the century's basic questions. The brutal fact of lambs turning into wolves, of respectable family fathers becoming assassins, has exposed fissures in humanity's aspect that can no longer be understood in Dostoevskian terms. It is the question posed by Büchner's Danton—"What is this thing inside us that lies, whores, steals, and murders?" The potential for negative unmasking is immanent in man, a permanent feature of his existence. A crucial point, however, will emerge subsequently. To Peter Weiss the excrescences of civilization, of a repressive society, seem to exist only in what he considers the "bourgeois" world.

His self-accusation as potential "persecutor" and "executioner" is a key to the author's entire work. Images of obsession, murder, shooting, and hanging multiply. The young man who had broken with his family, who had refuted middle-class security and intended to consecrate his life to his calling as an artist, now sees himself faced with another alternative: "The only milieu I had wanted was the one I created for myself. I had been allowed to cut out and make the most of it, or die in the attempt." But "leaving the family" does not bring the "creative explosions" he had anticipated. The "prodigal son" finally returns to the family "castle."

At this point the narrator discovers in Kafka's work a world that no longer knows the "chance of retreat." He

is alerted to the trial in which he himself is entrapped.
Like Kafka's heroes, he feels torn from a way of life
dictated by birth and destiny. He is unable either to penetrate or to interpret existence. But his encounter with
Kafka's writings teaches him more than the realization of
"impossibility and no way of escape."

The process of being wrenched away, the moment of
self-forgetfulness, the confrontation with the truth of being, leads the narrator—as it does Kafka's heroes—to
examine his life as if it were something alien.

The transition from universal law to autonomy, which
remains a utopian projection for Kafka, is realized in the
author's reflection, which is imbued with thoughts of
obsession. "The purpose of your survival may be to find
out where the evil lies and how to fight it. You are still
burdened with the ballast of your bourgeois origins. You
know it is all rotten and doomed to decay. Yet you do
not dare make a clean break with it. Your attempts at
work will be in vain as long as they do not contribute to
the struggle to remold society." Kafka's existential problem is overcome with the help of ideology. The "wall"
against which Kafka finally "battered himself to death"
consists, in the narrator's opinion, "of laws handed down"
which he thinks he can circumvent by a simple "step
sideways."

Before gaining distance from his own past, the
author, continually haunted by obsessions, must endure
periods of "discouragement," of "inability to work."

Finally he carries destruction to the point of deliberate self-abasement, thus experiencing release and a
new beginning. "This was the world of madness and I
could alter it . . . it had only eaten away the happy childhood years, but I could find other years, could discard
humbug and burst into the laughter of contempt that had
once previously been restrained." Laughter and change—
one leading to Marat and to the post-Marat period, the
other to Mockinpott and Sade.

In the spring of 1945 the narrator sees the end of

the "development" in which he had "grown up." The horror then being exposed to the eyes of the world, the sight of mountains of corpses, again poses the question: To whom does he now belong, as a living person, as a survivor? Has he been a passive victim or does his passivity rank him among the executioners? The step toward commitment leads to the rough recognition of his personal truth, self-analysis. Who was this self "laden . . . with dirt, with crap"?

The writings of Henry Miller deal the "death blow" to the world in which the author used to hold "dialogues with Kafka." Everything was "tangible and possible" in "the dazzlingly bright world of daylight" of *Tropic of Cancer*; "sex, which in Kafka lay dimly in the background, assumed a tropical luxuriance"; all that had been concealed is exposed. Instead of Kafka, it is Henry Miller now, and his rebellion against any form of authority. The author apparently failed to realize at the time that Miller is actually a product of this "corrupt civilization which was longing for death"—the unintentional reverse side of the coin, so to speak—while Kafka's K "struggles" for the right to be himself.

In the spring of 1947—after a failed marriage, an intense love relationship that ended soberly, and the vain attempt to conform—the narrator arrives at the moment of definite liberation. The wish expressed in *Leavetaking* to take "fate" into his own hands and to make "the fact of my not belonging a source of power for a new independence" has now become a reality.

In this sense the two autobiographical works refer to one another and join in a single perspective. Leaving home, self-liberation, and setting out for a life of his own—directed chiefly at the realm of feelings—was the condition for mental and artistic autonomy and self-discovery in language; this is the effort and aim that runs through *Vanishing Point*. In terms of perspective, the vanishing point is that point where straight parallel lines meet in infinity.

Both works have had to be presented in detail because they furnish the basic material, a kind of skeleton key, for Peter Weiss's later work. Perhaps one of Goethe's frequently quoted phrases may be used once more in the twentieth century, the one about "the great confession" of which his works were segments. It undeniably applies to few contemporary writers as much as to Peter Weiss.

The persona of this author as presented in his writing shows his subjective personal conflicts not only as typical of his time but also as a distinct reflection of universal problems. They are thus endowed with a unique prismatic quality, a relevance beyond agreement or contradiction. The result of functioning as a ready mirror is an expansion in scope and dimension, but the themes remain essentially uniform. The subject will invariably be liberation, rebellion—and revolution.

We noted at the outset that at the end of *Vanishing Point* the prodigal son is left with freedom and language as his sole possessions. To these must be added the awareness of guilt—an emotional reality which even freedom has not done away with. Together they are potential indicators of the future. The narrator feels guilty when, in 1945, he sees "the end of the development" in which he grew up; killing grounds, mountains of corpses, an informal world. He is guilty because he survived, because he knew and thought about "the misery of the world" in general terms, instead of risking his life, daring to change the world. He reproaches himself for not having mustered "the strength to rebel." The thought of childhood friends tortures him. In 1965 he once again speaks of the "great sin of omission" in a comparison of his own situation with that of Dante. "Who is my Beatrice?" he asks. A childhood love whom he had not dared approach. He was expelled, driven into exile; Beatrice remained behind. If he had had the courage, he would have taken her along on the flight. "Perhaps she was murdered, perhaps she was gassed."

They meet again in "paradise." But a modern Dante

can see Beatrice "only as a dead person"; for him a description of paradise would be "a description of the oppressed and the tortured."

Awareness of guilt leads to commitment. The writer becomes a "spokesman" and advocate. Kafka, with whom Weiss had identified at one time, becomes the representative of the "twisted, guilt-laden, doomed, and damned bourgeoisie," as he put it in *Partisan Review*.

A Survey of Hell:
The Shadow
of the Coachman's Body

"*Topographical instruments*," "road markers" to "indicate positions" is what Peter Weiss calls the words used by the writer who has severed all bonds. Language becomes a shell, a shelter. At the same time it allows for distance; it conjures up a world, but in so doing it protects from it. This is particularly true for the "micronovel" *Der Schatten des Körpers des Kutschers* (tr. *The Shadow of the Coachman's Body*).

In *Vanishing Point* Peter Weiss reports on a sojourn in the country, in a cottage in the woods, near a farm. The small enclosed world becomes for him a place of banishment and damnation. The narrator is reminded of Swedenborg's picture of hell. It is the "desire" to surrender to "banishment and damnation," to stagnation, to the other people who are hell, that keeps him in this world.

In *The Shadow* hell is no longer seen with the eyes of the suffering subject. It is surveyed, corroded by grotesquerie unmasked. The author uses language as art, a means of keeping the world at bay.

"Turning seeing into an occupation," the first-person narrator receives images of a house, its inhabitants, and its surroundings. Perhaps it is a farmhouse, perhaps a country inn. "Writing down observations" is the narrating I's description of his inventory. Its detachment and mimetic immediacy contrast in some instances with surrealist experiments.

Thirteen stages, using different observation posts—privy, attic room, kitchen, foyer, staircase, living room, courtyard, the doctor's room, the housekeeper's room—record both direct observations and subsequent recapitulations of any reality-constituting particulars that impinge on his perceptions, primarily his sense of sight and sound. Detail is placed next to detail. The author works like a sequence of photographic plates, technically precise, disinterested, a spectator and voyeur who is satisfying his idle curiosity and who—as Peter Weiss put it in an essay on avant-garde cinema—gauges a situation.

Dispassionately, even indifferently he describes a damaged world which conceals its infernal nature behind the mask of a bourgeois idyll. Description alternates with dream images, and the whole lies under a blanket of lifeless speculations which serve to emphasize its lack of familial ease. This is the same viewpoint from which Mockinpott, who tries in vain to discover the meaning of life, would have had to see the world had he been a writer.

Modifying the concept of the comic strip, the result can be called *grotesque strip*. The watching and waiting recorder captures on paper, not processes grasped by the senses, procured by a blunting and, as it were, falsifying general perspective, but events presented in isolation. Their flow is the result of memory and annotation. Weiss describes a reality which is half veiled to him but which he comes to recognize as "reality-in-itself" to the extent that he refrains from ascribing "meaning" to it. To Weiss, external order produces a deceptive semblance of meaning, while the apparent lack of organization is the raw material of the reality that is revealed to the eye and ear.

Peter Weiss's method, which may be called "severe, cold-blooded" in Alfred Döblin's words, is thus simply a continuation of techniques begun by Flaubert and Spielhagen, which sustained Naturalism, Expressionism, and Futurism, and continue today in the "nouveau roman."

Döblin—who, next to Carl Einstein, is the founder of an expressionist prose style—became a spokesman for the tradition of objectifying narrative. Self-effacement, authorial alienation, depersonalization are his most substantial requirements. He considers psychology "dilettantish guesswork," "abstract phantasmagoria," "sham lyricism"; the "theme" is nothing more than "poetic gloss." Writers should look to psychiatry instead, since it had long since recognized the naïveté of psychology and limited itself to "recording events—with a shake of the head and a shrug of the shoulders for the rest of the 'why' and 'how.'" The reader, not the author, should be the judge. For Döblin, the outward appearance of the novel can be stone or steel, electrically ablaze or somber; it is silent. In other words, the depicting author has no business standing between the reader and depicted world. He presents, shows what happens, completely relinquishing any attempt at motivation or explanation. His object is "lifeless" reality, presented in a "cinematic style" of the "utmost precision" and economy. Döblin's article "To Novelists and Their Critics," written in 1913, culminates in an appeal to "Courage for kinetic imagination and the recognition of the unbelievable factual outlines! Fact-fantasy!"

It is all the more surprising therefore that Alfred Döblin's name does not appear among the writers Weiss mentions in his autobiographical works. Around 1940 Weiss discovered "the twenties," as he writes in *Vanishing Point.* The art of that period contained values for him on which one could "elaborate." There is no question that Peter Weiss has "elaborated."

The prerequisites for Döblin's objectivist style consist of commenting narrator (previously Friedrich Spielhagen's *conditio sine qua non*), and absolute autonomy of the material itself—that is, the waiver of causality as the explanation for man and the world.

Weiss took a crucial further step. While in his early writings Döblin deposed the I and let the novel seemingly tell itself in the naturalist tradition even as he made use of imagined speech and inner monologue, Peter Weiss chooses the personal perspective, lending the narration a close system of coordinates and a center of orientation. His first-person narrator, who claims merely to record personal experiences—who, so to speak, cloaks the narrative in autobiography—replaces the seemingly scientific objectivity of epic narrative with the more modest, more honest "subjective" objectivity of a personal inability to know conditioned by the point of view. The result is a magnified authenticity. The notes no longer serve self-exploration and self-representation; rather they merge in a kind of "reel" record of the illumination of a field of vision or of hearing.

Verbs of hearing and seeing predominate, while verbs of inner perception have been dropped completely. The period which normally ends a prose work is also missing.* The process of documentation knows neither beginning nor end. Theoretically only the narrating I is imbued with unity and wholeness in the world of *The Shadow*; its instrument of perception is a geometric surveying point, controlled at the center, from which the (narrated) world is seen and heard.

As is the case in the works of Kafka, who places the burden of the distortion of the world presented in his work on the reader himself and holds him responsible by depriving him of the alibi of a mentally disturbed narrator, *The Shadow* produces an effect of inescapability. The reader feels compelled to take a stand although the narrative is objective and detached. He too has no alibi, since he is confronted with a flawless, honest, I-perspective, which neither distorts, nor omits but, on the contrary, presents intact the minute, precise, observations of the recording perception.

Since the author cannot be blamed for the reader's discomfort in the face of this reality, the threatening ele-

---

* The English translation unfortunately supplies a final punctuation mark, violating the author's intention. The same change occurs in the translation of *Conversation* (see below).

ment must be located either in the world or in the reader
himself. He finds himself in a reality in which objects
come dangerously alive, while life itself appears dissected
and grotesque, peopled with puppets. How does this
contradictory impression arise?

Peter Weiss has crossed a border. By attempting to
realize the demands of naturalism and its heritage in their
most extreme form, he carried the possibilities of objective description to the point of absurdity. Extreme precision turns out to be distortion. Seeing enables a perception of simultaneity, the grasping of adjacency, contemplation of objects existing side by side in a given space.
Articulated language is enumeration. It proceeds in sequence, one by one, point by point. In view of this essential difference, can an image of eye or ear be translated
into language should the author wish to dispense with
what he considers to be falsifying qualitative abstraction,
which corresponds to interpretation? Though Peter Weiss
wrote an essay entitled "Laokoon oder Über die Grenzen
der Sprache" (*"Laocoön, or On the Limits of Language"*), he hardly confronted the problem that had
prompted Lessing to write *Laocoön, or On the Limits of
Painting and Poetry."*

"Poetry," according to Lessing, "in her progressive
imitations, can only make use of one single property of
bodies [objects in a given space], and must therefore
choose that one which conveys to us the most sensible
idea of the form of the body, from that point of view for
which it employs it." But what happens when many bodies
side by side have many qualities, and the adjacency must
be rendered in the "objective" succession of the action?

The "co-existent element of the body" collides with
the "consecutive nature of speech." The result is dissolution, dispersion. "And it often happens," Lessing tells us,
"that we have forgotten the first line by the time we
arrive at the last," because the eye perceives at a glance,
but the poet "recounts it one by one, with remarkable
slowness." Balance and suspense are, in such cases, fur-

nished by meaningful comment; the narrator's interven-
tion closes the gaps and binds up the raw material of
life. The image of the whole owes its integration to the
cooperative action of both.

But what if a writer such as Peter Weiss has to describe an evening meal shared by six persons? What
happens if he attempts to describe the event with photographic precision? The collision mentioned by Lessing
occurs. Sixfold coexistence cannot be harmonized with
succession without the help of abstraction to gather the
disparate elements together. As long as a single line of
action is pursued and resolved in images, cinematic
sequence results; integration occurs automatically. But
when the reader must perceive a collective action—these
six persons, all eating dinner—quantitatively and qualita-
tively at the same time, without an abstracting merger of
the two, without simplifying generalization, spatial and
temporal interdependence must be disjoined and tele-
scoped in a ratio of six to one (six steps to the side, one
step forward). Six adjacent images must be aligned in
succession before the action, the true sequence, can continue. It is as though a film were to stop, then move
ahead with a sudden start—jerky, distorted, interspersed
with stills. The effect goes beyond alienation, it impinges
on the grotesquely comic. The alienated objects, stripped
of their context and frame of reference, become embodiments of the unknown, omens of darkness, danger, cruelty,
torture, and death. They elicit sensory impressions, they
unleash mystery, before sinking back into the ordinary.
Thus particles of reality, such as "sheath of a sword,"
"sheath," and "crowbar" can become sexual metaphors,
while "hatchet" and the figures of "father" and "coachman" become metaphors of violence, without the author's
explicit statement.

In Dali's sense of "critical paranoia," the object
becomes fully visible, thanks to the description; it becomes the "catalyst of manifold desires, longings, drives,
instincts"—and, we must add, of anxieties. For Boger

and his swing are no less present as associations than are
the gas chamber and death by suffocation. Because man
lives in an inhuman world, objects take on an inhuman
quality. But it is not the fault of the objects; it is man's
fault, because the light that falls upon the objects
emanates from him.

All these reflections lead to the conclusion that what
is new in the "esoteric" prose of *The Shadow* is not the
neosurrealist play with associations of images and words.
Rather it is the absurdly exaggerated refinement of the
naturalistic technique, the manic-detached record of
events, the exposure of the pores of a reality so imminent
that it confirms suspicion and knowledge, provokes fear
and repulsion. "Lifeless reality," conceived as meaningless and superreal, is resolved into the grotesque strip.

In the Soul Maze:
The Conversation of the Three Walkers

"*A soul maze*, a pit of feeling and thought" is Peter Weiss's name for the edifice of the mailman Cheval in his essay "Der grosse Traum des Briefträgers Cheval" ("The Grandiose Dream of Mailman Cheval"), written in 1960. The construction is meant to be the expression of a soul. Contemplating it, one is able to penetrate deeply into a person's "imaginary inner world." Everything the country mailman encounters on his rounds becomes material, "background for the flow of his imagination."

Any reader of *Das Gespräch der drei Gehenden* (tr. *The Conversation of the Three Walkers*), written in 1962, is reminded of the above essay. Flow constitutes the fundamental principle of *The Conversation*. The present participle in the German title indicates that the narrative situation (if that is to be the starting point) is resolved in motion. "They were just men who were walking walking walking"; the work begins almost like a fairy tale. Then the narrators are introduced; they are Abel, Babel, and Cabel, three men, wanderers "on the bridge," "in the park," who met by chance. Their names are ciphers, symbols of Everyman yet facets of a self.

The epic perspective of "they were" changes to a triple I and ends in the collective "we"—"we are walking walking walking." The past tense becomes the present, stressing the allegory. The three men have been brought together by the way over the "bridge," the walk from

shore to shore, from birth to death. The bridge is the
dominating symbol of the text; it is its theme.

Thirty prose sections are fitted into the flexible
frame; they are terse, sketchy, occasionally anecdotal.
They consist of stories, observations, experiences, and
visions representing dream images of anxieties and
desires, crucial events that hover between life and death.
Whichever one of the three men happens to be speaking
remains in semidarkness. They are layers, fragments of
an I; together they constitute a long interior monologue.
"I think this bridge must be new," says one. "The bridge
has been there a long time," begins another. "Yesterday
I rode on the ferry again," asserts the third. The effect
of such contradiction and simultaneity of points in time,
of planes, is timelessness. It transfers the events into a
floating realm beyond time. In German, there is no final
period. The fable can have no ending, no more than can
the flow of life that carries our images, dreams, and
ideas. Just as the narrators are on the move from shore to
shore, the stuff of their narration is also in motion; only
at the core does it coalesce into a tangible setpiece.

The organization of the work resembles that of a
mobile, offering ever new constellations, precise yet pointing beyond the moment and beyond themselves. The epic
structure of the narrative contributions by the first-person
narrators is heightened by the stories of the ferryman and
his six sons, which one of the three walkers tells. The
ferryman mentions three sons each time he conveys the
narrator across the river in the morning and evening.
Is this to be taken as a reference to Noah and his three
sons? Does the unchanging river conjure up primal time?
The ferryman Noah crossed the flood waters because "The
earth also was corrupt before God, and . . . filled with
violence." The world of that time is not so different from
the world of today. If the ferryman and his sons are seen
as representative of humanity, the stories the first-person
narrators tell about Jam, Jim, Jom, Jum, Jym—names

that are also ciphers, symbols—are confirmed and raised
to a higher power. Direct experience of the triple self and
the indirect world reflect and complement each other.

Comparison of the world depicted in *The Shadow*
and in *Leavetaking* and *Vanishing Point* to the prose of
The Conversation will not reveal anything essentially new.
The consecutive images of almost archetypal power do
not suffice to furnish the scene. Particles of a reality, they
may be characteristic of the memory and experience of
damaged existence. The imagination of disaster conjures
up nightmares, revealing a world of menace and pain.
Descriptions of torture, maiming, violence, and death
predominate. While nature as background and environment is depicted as idyllic, relationships among persons
and with things are determined by hostility and misunderstanding.

In this work, too, the author refrains from interpretation. The three first-person narrators contribute
their stories, which are sometimes detached, sometimes
sympathetic, sometimes fragmentary, sometimes the flesh-
ing out of sketches. Compared to *The Shadow*, narration
outweighs description, in accordance with the situation.
The narrative fabric, interwoven with patterns of reality
and imagination, is softer, more colorful, more musical.
It is a good, solid prose, recalling Hermann Hesse rather
than Döblin and the inventory of *The Shadow*. The contrast between circular rationality and flowing, luxuriant
imagination also recalls Surrealism and the movies associated with it.

In his long essay "Avantgarde Film" Peter Weiss
noted that, in contrast to films burdened with "so much
dialogue that tries to explain everything, with descriptions
of hermetic personalities, with plot complications and external motives for actions," avant-garde works try to
"express emotions and mental associations that are often
beyond the reach of reason." In other words, there is no
"solution." "Impulses" and dream images are evoked.

Compared to the psychic automatism of the Surrealists, however, the text of *The Conversation* may be more accurately defined as semiautomatic.

The Surrealist tradition begins to take on a crucial role only in Peter Weiss's later works. A precipitation of it in *The Conversation of the Three Walkers* appears mainly in the themes which recall such Surrealist films as those by Durand or René Clair.

In sum, the themes of these loosely connected sections —death, flight, pain, agony, suffering from a reality constantly turning into alienating "superreality"—are no more than variations on the fundamental dualism characteristic of Peter Weiss's work. The "walkers" move between the two poles because standing still is hell.

The Diagnosis of Society
as Surrealist Puppet Show:
The Insurance Policy

Peter Weiss's second dramatic work appeared in 1952, the same year in which he wrote *The Shadow of the Coachman's Body*. Unlike *The Tower*, written four years earlier, *Die Versicherung (The Insurance Policy)* deals, not with the self-analysis of "subjective drama," but with an analysis and disclosure of the order and living conditions in bourgeois society, where chaos and violence, repressed amorality and barbarism may at any time crack the shell of conformism.

In 1922 Yvan Goll announced the death of drama. Until he wrote its necrology Goll had actively represented Expressionism for seven years. But the "superrealism" he expounded thereafter still embodies Expressionist subject matter. His post-Expressionist grotesques relied less on the striving for form than on tendentiousness denoting social criticism, as became the case in the works of Peter Weiss. The intended effect is grotesque satire. The sham reality of ordinary middle-class life is to be disclosed by shock effects in order to expose the "superreal" reality concealed behind the sham.

"The tower . . . O where is the tower . . ." is the question at the end of *The Tower*. It is a promise of liberation. Four years later, in 1952, *The Insurance Policy* ends with a question and an answer. Alfons, the police commissioner, asks where he is being taken; where the likes of him belong, replies the policeman. There is no definition of what is meant by "where." Nor is Leo's, the

outsider's, threat more than empty rhetoric; it implies
only dissolution, not a new order. It refers to the chaos
devouring Western society, to anarchy.

The scene has shifted from the inner world of *The
Tower* to the social reality of the "late-capitalist countries," into rooms that give the illusion of prosperity but
are filled with poison and decay, avarice and envy; within
this torpid setting the inhabitants slowly slash at each
other, to use an image Peter Weiss applied to Strindberg
and to Sweden. Numbness and paralysis are the essential
qualities of hell, of the place that "bars evolution and
excludes all thought of change." In order to prevent any
misunderstanding as to his intention—the description of
the fall of a bourgeois Gomorrah—the author remarks in
a note, "The anarchist-prerevolutionary atmosphere of the
play may be made topical by including recent events in
the late-capitalist countries. The action can, for instance,
be moved to the United States, and the names of the characters Americanized."

The play consists of nineteen set pieces, its reasons
for being stated in the title. Like epic theater, it provides
an ironical foretaste of the play's direction and contents.
It begins with the arrival of guests at Alfons's home.
They have come to help Alfons and his wife Erna cele-
brate the final signing of an insurance policy. These
representatives of a bourgeois world, seemingly intact,
gather to confirm and increase its security with the symbolic act of taking out insurance.

The superficial impression created by evening gowns,
white ties and tails, decorations, ceremonious introduc-
tions, and pantomimed conversation reflects a sham world
of crumbling deception, which shows its true face in the
following scenes, when damned-up reality breaks through.
Repressed facts come to light, unleashed cruelty and
primitive sexuality burst forth, drawing everything into
a grotesque, destructive vortex.

No sooner have the guests sat down on the sketchy

accommodations provided in the opening scene than the
commissioner announces the reason for the party. Since
there is no way of knowing what disasters and revolutions the future may bring, awareness of his responsibility
as a "husband, property owner, and citizen" prompts him
to take out insurance.

One of the guests is Dr. Kübel, who brings along his
assistant, Grudek, dressed in a chauffeur's uniform.
Kübel himself, wearing a cape and top hat, looks like a
figure from a horror movie. When someone almost chokes
on a bone, Kübel lures them all to his private clinic,
where the second scene is set.

In the clinic, the guests are made to undress. Alfons,
with suicidal persistence, continues his discussion with
the directors of the insurance company. While the ad-
vantages and guarantees of the policy are being explored,
the mood becomes sinister. As is the case in the later
Marat/Sade, words and concepts are grotesquely refuted
by events. While the attendants in "Doctor Kübel's Private
Clinic—All Types of Cures" get ready to administer the
"treatments," the head of the insurance company reads
aloud from the policy, enumerating the hazards against
which the police commissioner has been insured. The
play represents the dismantling of the seemingly secure
position, it demolishes "assurance." Although the conversation is about security, insecurity grows just as in
Marat/Sade revolution is the constant subject while the
Restoration triumphs all around.

Alfons signs the document and, pursued by storms
and lightning flashes, flees by means of a ladder in the
third scene. The fourth reveals Dr. Kübel's private clinic
to be a torture chamber. The sixth scene shows Kübel
in his chaotic lower-middle-class home, eating (burned)
pudding. Leo—who, clad in red fur, had symbolized
anarchic animal drives in the opening scene, at the time
the party moved to the clinic—is lying in the bathtub.
Now, if not sooner, it becomes clear that the same con-

nection exists among Kübel's torture chambers, cruelty, and unbridled sexuality as is shown later to prevail in *Marat/Sade* and the world of the concentration camps.

The name Leo is an unmistakable allusion to the "lion" in *The Tower*, which symbolizes wild, untamed power. In essence, Dr. Kübel and Leo are one and the same character, to be considered as alter egos. Leo represents the unleashed drive toward elemental chaos and vital, liberating anarchy, while crippling destructive drives and loathsome unsatisfied longing, expressed through cruelty, predominate in Dr. Kübel and in his assistant, Grudek. Thus they represent two extremes—bourgeois-fascist behavior and aimless, anarchic ramblings. Kübel's personality is made sufficiently clear in his remarks about art while looking through one of Leo's books. He admires bourgeois realism showing underwear and garters, the lascivious, cheap, dishonest, "beautiful" like the official art of the Third Reich.

Following the seventh scene which, like the twelfth consists exclusively of visual and sound effects, the eight and succeeding scenes show the unleashed forces reaching several climaxes of horrible, disgusting, animal-like, "liberating" copulations, of addiction to instincts, of brutality and hypocrisy. In the ninth scene, for example, the effects, straight out of Punch and Judy, end in a grotesque parallel action. While downstairs a body falls dully to the floor, the wife sends whispered words of love after Leo, who has fled up the stairs.

Meanwhile, the clinic treatment continues in the thirteenth scene. There are injections and tortures; the "attendants" do their lasciviously cruel "duty." The analogy with the world of the concentration camps is all too obvious, underlined by the patient's incapacity to understand what is happening and to transform the collective suffering into the collective action of rebellion. Individual cruelty and bestial copulation add to the organized terror. Humiliation abounds, pain is inflicted either in conjunction with lust or purely for the sake of cruelty.

The fifteenth scene uses the simultaneity of three interlocked settings. The owner of the casino—another one of the guests at the feast—pushes his way into a cage, among goats kept as test animals, to the feeding trough. Like the other prisoners he begs to be set free, since he has done nothing; he argues absurdly that he must get to his "art collection." Grudek, wearing a doctor's white coat, refuses this request and exhorts the guest to follow the example of the forbearing animals. At the same time Erna is discovered under the trash heap, in the arms of a garbage collector, while Alfons cuddles with Hulda, who combines the roles of maid and nurse. At the end of the simultaneous scenes the owner of the casino, who vainly screams for Alfons, is driven "to work"; Erna, who moans for her husband and her children, is carted away; and Hulda leads the police commissioner to the hairdresser to be "leveled."

Two scenes later Leo proclaims the revolution while buildings collapse and jets roar overhead. The police commissioner, who had found consolation with Hulda, is "dismantled" with her help. Even his children no longer recognize him. The man's claim to be the police commissioner is greeted with laughter. He no longer understands the world. "While policemen forcibly drag Alfons off to the left and he disappears," the final stage direction reads, "Hulda and Grudek walk past downstage, from left to right. They stroll along laughing. Hulda rotates her parasol. The sewing machines hum." What difference is there between these two and Alfons, the toppled dictator?

This brief summary indicates the way the play combines the intention to shock by means of ridicule—as postulated by Goll—with the release of drives and a portrayal of the bourgeois world as a universe of fascist terror. Repressed reality is revealed in imagery and action. The result links the bourgeois world with the world of the concentration camp as the two sides of the same coin. Weiss offers no clear alternatives. Revolution is still defined as pure anarchy, as freedom "from" but not yet as

freedom "to." Ideology appear only in the evaluation and
description of bourgeois society; it does not yet offer
a choice. Dissolution takes the place of change.

Although Weiss's antibourgeois bias is not yet expressed as commitment to a particular ideology, the play
nonetheless contains elements of his later "partisan"
documentary theater. Thus, true to the basic concepts of
Piscator's "political extravaganza," projections, adver-
tisements, and news headlines are introduced in order to
raise the "private scenes to historical . . . political, economic, social" dimensions, to establish a relationship
between injustice, cruelty, and sexuality and the existing
social order.

The world of Dr. Kübel's private clinic, in which the
members of the dinner party are deprived of their identi-
ties by a "process of dehumanization," is dominated by
two figures who are both among the oppressed. The rule
of terror practiced by the maid Hulda and the chauffeur
Grudek—who, disguised as a doctor, fatally tortures one
of the captive women with instruments reminiscent of the
Middle Ages—foreshadows the scenes in Weiss's play
about Auschwitz in which doctors who are not doctors
also put prisoners to death even while they assure them
that they are helping. The self-analytical question about
the "role" to be played by captive and guard is raised,
though "unmasked" society is not yet hailed into court.
The author limits himself to showing its dissolution and
fall. This "surrealist-visionary form of drama," as Weiss
calls it, is characterized by torture and destruction, released inhibitions, and pleasure in decay.

The author's interest in Surrealism and especially
in the Surrealist cinema unquestionably influenced the
writing of this Surrealist grotesque. "Hulda rotates her
parasol. The sewing machines hum" are the closing words
of the play. If the dissection table in Dr. Kübel's "private
clinic" is added to the other props (of which the "sewing
machine" is reminiscent of Schwitters's "Merzbühne"),
another allusion to Surrealism is established. In the essay

"Avantgardefilm," cited above, Weiss recalls Lautréamont's famous aphorism—"As wonderful as the chance
encounter of a sewing machine and an umbrella on a
dissection table." We will return to the theme of Surrealism in our discussion of *Marat/Sade*.

The relationship of *The Insurance Policy*—or *The
Insecurity Policy*, as it might more properly be called—
to the "oratorio" *The Investigation* is the same as that of
The Tower to *Leavetaking* and *Vanishing Point*. Both
cases show that, since objective reality as such has revealed itself as absurdity, the individual-aesthetic and the
collective-political components that make up the reality
of contemporary life can be portrayed as such—that is,
by describing society with all its paradoxes—rather than
by hyperbolic and allegorical superlatives.

The Play of Kaspar Rosenrot:
Night With Guests

Certain aspects of *The Insurance Policy* are reminiscent of Alfred Jarry's *Ubu Roi and* Punch and Judy shows. The masklike nature of the characters, the absence of inner motivation, the stylization of the action, the inclusion of "big dolls," mechanical cruelty—all these recall the Surrealist theater derived from Jarry and the extra-literary tradition of the puppet show. The scene in which Dr. Kübel shows his true face and subjects the guests to inhuman tortures in his hospital, for instance, has its place in the tradition of *Moritat* (tabloid ballad) and, as mentioned above, horror movies. There is a direct line from this to *Marat/Sade* by way of the blood-curdling play *Nacht mit Gästen* (tr. *A Night with Guests*). In his afterword to this play Weiss reminisces about the puppet theater and concludes that the play belongs to a form of theater which he would like to "revive"—the show booth.

It is characteristic of this type of theater, which draws directly from the realm of the emotions, that it lays bare the hypocrisy of society, as was also Weiss's intention in *The Insurance Policy.*

Because the afterword originally made no mention of the serious, didactic purpose connected with these performances of songs and sensational tales, Weiss added a final moral for the 1963 Berlin première of the play, which had been written in the period 1962–1963, ideologizing it, in retrospect so to speak, and imposing a political position on a work of dramatic art.

Night with Guests consists of approximately six hundred rhymed couplets and quatrains. The subtitle calls it a ballad play. The action is as brutal as it is primitive. There are six characters: husband and wife, the actual victims; good "Peter Kruse with his red blouse," a rescuer and cautioning figure; "Kaspar Rosenrot, with my knife I'll cut your throat"; and the two youngsters, whose childish rhymes underscore the horror of the events.

While the husband and wife become alarmed, thinking that they hear footsteps, the children chant their nonsense rhymes. The effect is one of alienation, grotesquely distorting the action. Instead of Peter Kruse, it is Kaspar Rosenrot who appears in the house. The parents beg for mercy, they try to placate the murderer. But the intruder remains stolid and implacable; he sharpens his knife. Finally the husband offers him a chest full of gold which, he says, lies buried in the reeds near the lake. But he needs Kaspar's help to find it. Kaspar orders the husband to tie up his wife and to go and find the treasure chest by himself; before the husband goes, he admonishes the children to be nice to the guest.

While waiting for the father to come back, the children—strangely indifferent but adjusting to the situation—urge "Daddy Rosenrot" to remain and take their father's place. The wife offers him her bed. Kaspar eventually cuts the wife loose and retires for the night after the children have undressed him. Still holding his knife, he takes the wife with him.

At this point Peter Kruse enters the action. The door is open and he is about to go in when the husband returns with the chest. Kruse stabs him, thinking that he is a robber; at the same instant Rosenrot kills the wife.

Now robber and rescuer confront each other, the box of gold between them. They kill each other in the ensuing struggle. This final scene of violent death is to be performed Kabuki style, the acrobatic control of movements resembling a ballet. In the meantime the children

sneak away, unmoved, as though the adults' brawls did
not concern them in the least.

Thus ends the tale of horror. But there is a danger
that it will be misunderstood, that "Kaspar Rosenrot, I'll
cut your throat" will be seen only as the outsider, the
asocial animal, a universal type. The play would then be
dealing with the familiar, not very original farce of mis-
taken identity, a stock-in-trade of the Punch and Judy
show that never fails to get a laugh. But Weiss wants his
play to be interpreted on a social and political plane. As
already mentioned, he added a "moral" for the Berlin
première which is mentioned only in the epilogue. "Be-
hold the outcome of our fate / They lie, stabbed by a
fatal knife / the killers, husband, and the wife. By gold
we were destroyed, / for gold we now have died."

Meant as an ordinary puppet show, intended as
social criticism, the play is directed at the breakdown of
values and the constant potential for compromise. To save
their lives, the couple invite the murderer to dinner. The
children are immediately willing to accept the new
"father." The wife has no major objection to going to bed
with him. And what about the murderous burglar? Not
even he is able to pass up an opportunity; he accepts the
offer, knife in hand. But the instinctual coupling will not
prevent his stabbing the wife in cold blood.

The criminal shares the desires of the solid citizen—
who, in turn, tries to deceive the intruder. The children,
who are almost neutral in spite of their apparent readiness
to collaborate, are holding a "pink bow," eager to adorn
the newcomer with it—"You know what I mean." Does
that make them potential criminals? Are the husband
and wife criminals because they defend themselves, because they try to survive by any means at their disposal?
It would be foolish in such a context to speak of corruption or of sick, decadent behavior. The moral, then, is
clear. Since the criminal wants to be a solid citizen and the
solid citizen is potentially criminal, social conditions must
be changed to put a stop to it all. The action of *Night*

with Guests is as inconclusive as the tacked-on ending. The banal horrors, the dull mechanics of death, the understandable urge to survive—the reason for the family's accepting the killers, rather than any affinity between solid citizen and criminal—these are not enough to arouse the audience's interest, still less its sympathy.

The only striking element is the children's strange indifference. It is no different from that of the children in *The Insurance Policy*, who refuse to be "disturbed" and stubbornly carry on their games in spite of adults' shenanigans. Is this simply an effect devised for the sake of a stronger contrast, or did Weiss mean to suggest that the next generation will keep its distance from the fathers' society because it is not corrupted by "gold"? Can the author's reserved attitude toward his own moral really be taken seriously? In view of the 1968 epilogue to *The Insurance Policy*, according to which that play "has been actualized by recent events in the late-capitalist countries," one may be entitled to doubt it.

In this ballad play gold stands for capitalism. Senseless killing and corruption as the response to menace have their common origin, as Peter Weiss never tired of proving, in a social structure that becomes further and further reduced to a diabolical counterprinciple.

Interestingly, Peter Weiss accounts for his attraction to this type of theater with the fact, among others, that it has "no complications" and "does not depict souls"; "problems" are solved with "blows and knives." It offers a tangible, unambiguous world which has become fathomable again. In *Vanishing Point* Weiss spoke of the "making" of such a world as "a great adventure." The replacement of debate with violence is a familiar alternative not only because of Futurism and the Zen Buddhist masters. In the plays that follow *The Investigation*, erroneously called "documentary theater" (skipping the dialectic of *Marat/Sade*), Peter Weiss elevates this method to a principle. The passage is marked by Manichean dualism and loss of dialogue.

Job's Clownish Retreat
from the Quest for Meaning:
Mockinpott

Wie dem Herrn Mockinpott das Leiden ausgetrieben wird (tr. *How Mr. Mockinpott Was Cured of His Sufferings*) —a harlequinade in rhymed couplets begun in 1963 and finished in 1968—also sets out to solve the problems of this world by the method mentioned in *Night with Guests* —that is, with "blows and knives."

It is a "play in eleven scenes," with elements of both Punch and Judy shows and *commedia dell'arte*. Satirical buffoonery demonstrates a cure for the Kafkaesque-labyrinthine analysis of reality: by removing or altering the organs involved. If the world cannot be changed, we have the option of changing our emotional structure in order to make the world palatable.

The opening scene reveals Mockinpott in jail. Like Joseph K. in Kafka's *Trial*, he has been arrested though neither he nor his jailer knows the reason why. In prison, his complete loss of rights is aggravated by exploitation. After the captive is thoroughly fleeced and made to pay for "sponging on the state quite cheerfully," though everything seems to indicate that he is not guilty of anything (who is not reminded of the Nazi judicial practice that arbitrarily condemned people to death and assessed them for their own execution?), he is literally thrown out of the cell.

Shortly before his dismissal, two angels appear to the prisoner who would "like to know" the original question of the human creature. Their words place an absurd eschatological meaning on the action; Mockinpott must walk the painful road because he cannot "get the drift" of his "sufferings." And the reason he cannot "get the drift" is precisely because he asks for meaning—a necessity for him because he has been so badly dealt with. It is a vicious circle. To Mockinpott it is an obvious premise that everything that is happening in the world, everything that people do to other people, must have a meaning of which one can "get the drift."

At this early point two roads lie open. One, taken by the play, is the amputation of the need for meaning and its resolution into laughter; the other is escape into a new meaningfulness, a different lawfulness that leads almost automatically to a better world, the faith in a new Messiah.

In the second scene Jack Pudding makes his entrance. He is the cunning trickster who has long been a favorite of folk theater, a cheerful, honest fellow without a worry in the world. He arouses in Mockinpott the hope for understanding; but Pudding does not believe him either. Mockinpott goes home to his wife (third scene). Another man is with her. Mockinpott has obviously been replaced —a circumstance that allows Weiss to stage a variety of farcical devices. The angels, who return at regular intervals, contribute their devout comments. The punishment for Mockinpott's rebellion, his Luciferlike quest for meaning, increases.

His next visit, in the fourth scene, is to his boss, who chases him away. No one believes in his innocence. He left his workplace without permission, they logically point out. Pudding has a pat answer for Mockinpott who is now "in the open air" in the fifth scene. "Clearly it can't have been *your* job in any case / if there's another man now filling your place." Thus, unlike Mockinpott, he does not search for meaning and relies on the unquestioning alibi that there "must be a reason" for everything.

This leads to the sixth scene, "At the surgery." Pudding is convinced that Mockinpott is "ill" and that the doctor will be able to help him. The angels' comment undergoes a slight change. They say that "our good man" is "not yet" able to understand his suffering, thus hinting at the conclusion that understanding means not to question.

The climax and turning point of the play is a farcical operation, a bloody grotesque with burlesque overtones. The doctor opens Mockinpott's skull, pulls his heart out of his trousers, and after various procedures finally declares the patient cured. Instead of bemoaning his fate, as before, Mockinpott now bursts into giggles. He laughs out loud. To complete the picture, the angels appear, also jubilant.

In the eighth scene Mockinpott calls on the government. The reply to his reasonable, pertinent questions is a random gibberish—nonsense, garbled phrases, and clichés. Mockinpott is now about to track down the truth. Although (in the ninth scene) he still worries about where to turn if nobody will tell him right from wrong, he has already begun to give up thinking. The angels confirm that he is now very close to the explanation of his suffering and that God Himself will honor him with an appearance.

The tenth scene is titled "With Dear God." The ruler of heaven is clad in a "long fur coat"; he wears a "top hat" and "puffs at a fat cigar"; he is the prototypical capitalist. It turns out that even the good Lord does not know to what extent "the business" is still solvent. Heaven is a commercial enterprise. Mockinpott becomes furious and accuses God of being responsible for injustice and suffering—and thereby he is cured, enlightened. He realizes that it is meaningless to search for meaning.

In their final appearance, in the eleventh scene, the angels confirm that he has now grasped the nature of creation. According to them, he is now relieved of all suffering. Mockinpott has become the perfect puppet. He is in harmony with himself and with the world because he has learned to entrust himself to externalized directions. In the author's striking image, he used to mistake his right and left shoe, and as long as he kept asking for "meaning," he was unable to put on his boots properly. Now, in the final scene, he succeeds effortlessly, as a matter of course. The reduction has given him back equilibrium and grace. With "airy lightness, like a dancer, like a skater, he departs."

It is not by accident that Mockinpott meets Pudding after his release from prison. He is hungry, whereas Pudding has everything he needs. The name "Pudding," beyond being an allusion to the harlequinade and the *commedia dell'arte*, also indicates an attitude of uncaring, of indifference. Like Carlo and Pablo, like Jacques and the narrator of *Leavetaking*, and like Marat and Sade, Mockinpott and Pudding represent two developmental stages of one and the same character. Pudding is Mockinpott's alter ego; he embodies the qualities that allow for survival in the world. At the end, therefore, Mockinpott is able to leave while Pudding lies flat on his back, snoring. Mockinpott has caught up with him and surpassed him. The struggle for meaning and identity has been replaced by the joyful denial of any possibility of realization and understanding—"understanding" being the attempt to discover "meaning" behind a word or an action—in short, nihilism.

Nihilism, one might say, in the Nietzschean sense represents the prerequisite for the step, or leap, into a different kind of faith, a new meaningfulness that marks Peter Weiss's work after *Marat/Sade*. It must be remembered that *Mockinpott*, begun in 1963 along with *Marat/Sade*, was finished in 1968, when the author had completed work on *The Investigation, Gesang vom Lusitanischen Popanz* (tr. *Song of the Lusitanian Bogey*), and *Discourse on Viet Nam*. At the same time, in his essay "Das Material und die Modelle. Notizen zum dokumentarischen Theater" ("Material and Models. Notes on Documentary Theater"), Weiss opposed the "concept of an absurd and hopeless world" and expressed the view that reality, unfathomable as it might seem, could none-theless be explained in every detail.

Thus this tabloid ballad makes a harlequinade of the conflict between individual freedom and social—that is, bourgeois-social—terror. We are not given the didactic result; social criticism is satisfied with the demonstration of a horrible, absurd example. Job or Lazarus becomes Everyman in the garb of a clown; they heal their wounds by ignoring them.

Is freedom a fiction? If the perception of its possi-bilities leads to the results shown by Mockinpott's ex-periences, we are left with a choice between resignation, fatalistic acceptance, and hope based on a mechanistic-materialistic order. Mockinpott could be cured through either, since both relieve him of the quest for meaning.

Freud versus Marx,
or "Copulation"
and "Revolution":
Marat / Sade

Ceasing to search for the meaning of human existence had
relieved Mockinpott of his sufferings. The rest is laughter.
The play *Marat/Sade* also ends in laughter. The author
of the play within the play, the Marquis de Sade, laughs
at his own creatures. But his laughter is the laughter of
a man who knows; his resignation is that of a man who
has thought, believed, and fought before retreating into
laughter, before countering the world with art. The play
is the justification of a reformer who has failed; it is a
rebellious answer to questions that are at the same time
questions of principle.

The two-act play *Die Verfolgung und Ermordung
Jean Paul Marats dargestellt durch die Schauspieler-
gruppe des Hospizes zu Charenton unter Anleitung des
Herrn de Sade* (tr. *The Persecution and Assassination of
Jean-Paul Marat As Performed by the Inmates of the
Asylum at Charenton Under the Direction of the Marquis
de Sade*), begun as a work for radio, is set in a lunatic
asylum. The narrator of *Leavetaking* relates an early
memory of the "mental defectives" the child used to see
walking in the park. The sickness of disillusionment, impotence, and suspicion in which he took refuge lead to
his identification with the inmates of the asylum. It is
here that mental association first appears from the quest
for "liberation" through escape into illness and the
"asylum." Peter Weiss has given a precise definition of

51

what is meant by "asylum." It is a "hell," permanent
"residence in a penal institution." And hell is "paralysis,"
the place where no further development can occur, the
place that excludes all thought of change. In *The Shadow
of the Coachman's Body* Peter Weiss described such a
place of damnation in keeping with Swedenborg's (and
Strindberg's) concept of "hell." Other descriptions
abound in his subsequent works.

Sade's subjective opposition to the conditions of
society, which must appear to him in the light of the
asylum image, corresponds to the actual fact of the asylum
as a means of political pressure, as it is practiced to this
day. Imagination is outdone by reality. It is at this point
that *Marat/Sade* constitutes the link between Surrealist
grotesque and documentary theater. The work is composed on three levels. The play (showing the assassination of Marat) is performed as a play (by Sade) in the
play (by Peter Weiss). The three levels are paralleled
by the triple structure of time, place, and action.

Time. (1) The play takes place on July 13, 1793,
the day of Marat's assassination. (2) The play takes place
in 1808, staged by Sade, using the inmates of Charenton.
(3) The play is interpreted by the herald, the four
singers, Roux, and Coulmier, not only for the inmates and
the personnel of the institution, but also for contemporary
audiences.

Place. (1) The play is set in Paris. (2) Sade's production of the play takes place in Charenton. (3) The play
occurs in any theater where Peter Weiss's work is being
produced.

Action. (1) The play deals with the assassination of
Marat (1793, 1808, and today). (2) The play centers on
the dialogue between Marat and Sade (1808 and today).
(3) The play is framed by Coulmier and other com-
mentators (1808 and today).

These three levels are also mirrored in the triple
division of the play from a thematic and dramatic aspect.
The works consists of (1) a dramatic event which is its

subject, (2) turned by Sade into a play along the concepts of the theater of cruelty—specifically sadistic, perhaps—and (3) the production, or performance of these two aspects as a tabloid ballad play.

Peter Weiss applies his Chinese-box technique to historical events. The Marquis de Sade actually was confined at Charenton from 1803 until his death, and he really did write and stage plays with the inmates. On the other hand, the author's use of this type of montage succeeds in achieving a surrealist effect with the factual elements.

The play takes place on July 13, 1808, fifteen years after the assassination of Marat, at a time when the revolutionary uprising was giving way to Napoleon's enlightened depotism. The revolution is over. Have its ideas triumphed? Did they create a new reality? Did the mass sacrifices made in their name deprive them of their incentive? To the many questions there are many answers. Peter Weiss offers three of them in his play—three convictions, three reactions.

Sade has despaired of the revolution with which he had initially sympathized; he has seen through its contradictions and has withdrawn into his individuality. Resigned, he justifies his noninvolvement during his encounter with Marat. For Roux, the radical socialist and passionate pacifist, who is a kind of successor to Marat though he surpasses him in radicality, the idea of the revolution is eternal. A political prisoner in the asylum, he relives the revolution in Sade's play and is inspired by it to demonstrate his utopian faith and indestructible hope. Both are contrasted with Coulmier, the representative of the government, which owns the establishment where the performance takes place. He represents the perversion of the revolution while seeming to be its embodiment. The *conditio sine qua non* of all three is Marat, whose death is being enacted on stage. He is the nucleus, the symbol of the revolution, and in particular Sade's participation in it.

The characters—among whom Marat and Sade, because of their opposition, constitute the skeleton of the dramatic action—can be divided into three basic attitudes: (1) a revolutionary, socially committed group: Marat and Roux; (2) one individualist: Sade; and (3) a reactionary or counter-revolutionary group: Coulmier and Duperret. Between the first and the second group stand the four singers; between the second and the third stands Charlotte Corday. The herald, an atheist and follower of the revolution, functions as assistant director, presenting the events in ballad style at the request of the author and director, Sade. This device allows for a harlequinesque splitting of his personality.

It is well known that Jean-Paul Marat, a teacher of languages, writer, physician, and politician, was one of the most radical populist leaders of the revolution of 1789, and that he was stabbed to death on July 13, 1793, by Charlotte Corday. The Marquis de Sade, born in 1740, was imprisoned in 1801 because of his writings. In 1803 his family managed to have him transferred to the asylum at Charenton, where he died in 1814. His anarchistic individualism, his belief that literature must describe everything, even the greatest horrors, because they were intended by nature and were a part of the "natural man," made him a forerunner of nineteenth-century theories.

Sade's concept of man's right to absolute egotism seemed monstrous in his time. His linking of the unleashing of instincts with cruelty, of sensuality with violence strikes us today as typical of our day.

Sade joined the cause of the revolution, working among other things for reform of Parisian hospitals. He was appointed by the Health Committee to oversee hospital services and became chairman of the Piques Assembly (a ward committee) in 1793, two days before the assassination of Marat. In reality no conversation between Marat and Sade ever took place. Another historical fact of interest in this connection is that during his internment at Charenton, Sade was asked by Coulmier,

the director of the institution, to write and stage plays
with the patients.

The play is nevertheless neither a historical work
nor a dramatization of a historical theme. The only important point, however, is that the ideologies presented
on the stage are based on historical events which lend
them authenticity. The acts are broken down into thirty-
three scenes, some of which consist only of stage directions, such as scenes 1 and 3, or of a single sound, such as
scene 32. The division into scenes has a rhythmic rather
than a structural effect.

The play begins (scene 1) when the participants,
actors, sisters, and male nurses, walk on and take their
positions on stage—that is, in the bathhall of the asylum
of Charenton. In scene 2, Coulmier welcomes the visitors
and announces that the play is the creation of Monsieur de
Sade, "one of our residents." He combines his introduction with some broad references when he speaks of the
progress which his institution has made. "We're modern
enlightened and we don't agree / with locking up patients
We prefer therapy / through education and especially
art / so that our hospital may play its part / faithfully
following according to our lights / the Declaration of
Human Rights."

After the principal performers take their places
(scene 3), the herald—who comports himself like a
carnival barker—introduces each person and explains the
situation as it is historically known. The date he cites—
July 13, 1808—points to the coincidence of three time
levels: 1793, 1808, and the date of the particular performance in the present. This stratification is mirrored in the
fragmentation and simultaneity of the dramatic parts—as
indicated above—which may be subdivided into single
parts and double parts. The single parts include Sade and
Coulmier; the double parts are Marat, Roux (who is
confined because of political radicalism), Charlotte
Corday, and others.

The homage to Marat, performed in scene 5 by the

four singers and by the chorus—representing the fickle
voice of the people, in contrast to the anarchically im-
pudent four soloists—is also an indictment of postrevolutionary society. "Marat," they accuse, "we're poor and
the poor stay poor / Marat don't make us wait any
more / We want our rights and we don't care how / We
want our revolution *NOW*." The stage roles fuse with the
roles in real life. The level of the play as recreated history
fuses with that of performed reality. Criticism of the
postrevolutionary society makes itself heard and extends
the play beyond Sade's intentions, heightening the effect
of illusion by an appearance of "life."

Meanwhile Charlotte Corday enters (in scene 7),
played by a somnambulist. The sisters prepare her for
the first of her three visits and lead her downstage. She
accuses Marat, who is played by a paranoiac, of "spurt-
ing" poison from his "hiding place," of poisoning "the
people," of arousing them to "looting and murder." In
scene 8 Marat finds the time to proclaim that he is "the
revolution," that the others are only "hypocrites" sporting
"the people's cap." During this lament, and the affirmation that "thousands" of corpses are still not enough, the
four singers sit on the floor and play cards. They pay no
attention to Marat, because they see the play as play, as a
substitute for action. They are skeptics "with empty
stomachs." Their attitude is related to that of Sade and
yet its opposite. Sade salvages his revolution—which has
exposed the contradiction between "the natural instinctual
man" and the rational individual in the form of "mass
sadism"—by taking it to the safety of aestheticism,
whereas the four singers safeguard their revolution
through anarchy, which annuls the contradictions of the
revolution as much as does the game of art. Skepticism
and laughter are their chief reaction, as they are Sade's;
they have no illusions left when it comes to phrasemongering.

The moment has come for the central action—for
Charlotte Corday's visit and the murder. The stage direc-

tions indicate that Corday's performance "resembles a
ritual act." Song and pantomime are used in scene 10
to show Corday's arrival in Paris. The purchase of the
knife, with erotic overtones, and the depiction of life in
the Parisian alleys develops into a dance of death. Two
patients mime the guillotine. Preparations are under way
for an execution. Scene 11, titled "Death's Triumph,"
pantomimes an execution. Marat feels compelled to justify
the massacres and revenge by accusing those who drove
the executioners to the job. As might be expected, Coulmier intervenes; he feels that this is going too far. Sade
has no reaction. He gazes across the stage "with a mocking smile." His remark that the former possessors of all
earthly goods are turning their defeat into victory, and
that the guillotine saves them from endless boredom leads
to the central "Conversation Concerning Life and Death,"
in scene 12. The actions, pantomimes, and choral commentary are basically nothing more than a dramatic em-
bellishment of this core dialogue.

While the sisters murmur a "short litany," Marat
speaks "to Sade across the empty arena": "I read in
your books de Sade / in one of your immortal works /
that the basis of all life is death." Sade explains his own
attitude by his feelings about death. Man is both the
creation and the victim of nature, which devours him
without feeling, in total indifference. For this reason Sade
hates nature which denies all freedom to man, for
"natural man" whose drives have been released, is thereby
condemned to experience a new dependence—on nature
and his drives.

Physical release leads back into slavery almost as
much as does *intellectual* release, because universal freedom means replacing the notion of freedom with that of
the general will. The demand to submit to the wish of the
people also amounts to a negation of freedom. The result
of such a realization is the feeling of isolation and inevitability; it is the awareness of the absurdity of human
existence. The Marquis de Sade who is speaking here

has been frightened out of his dreams by experiencing
"mass sadism" and the general will—two phenomena that
call for freedom while at the same time negating it. Reality
has channeled as well as deepened his imagination, turning it into literature.

In death, the negation of life, Sade saw a means of
"extinguishing" nature. Nature the executioner is confronted by her pupil and conqueror, man the killer. Man
massacres, tortures, behaves perhaps "unnaturally" by
society's standards, in order to establish his freedom, his
independence of nature. This purpose requires a victim;
that is, man needs power and the presence of weak, defenseless beings who serve as objects of freedom-confirm-
ing killing or of a subject's cruelty. The abolition of class
distinctions, the even-handed distribution of power, its
"socialization," on the other hand, negate this possibility.

In this fashion the execution of Damiens, which
the author describes in full detail, becomes a passionate,
freedom-promoting act, compared to which "anonymous
cheapened death" by guillotine is nothing but empty
routine. Absolute revolution must remain a theoretical,
a personal fantasy that cannot be put into practice.

"For you just as for me," Sade says to Marat, "only
the most extreme actions matter." The revolution has
taught him that killing as a "proof" of "existence" and
freedom—*neco ergo sum*—can only be an idea, an individual concept, which can be realized in art but not as a
social idea or political action. Art and revolution are two
different matters, although they may be mutually related
so that the action that would otherwise die and fade away
may continue to exist as art. Marat opposes "action" to
Sade's withdrawal into the self in response to "Nature's
indifference." "I don't watch unmoved / I intervene / and
say that this and this are wrong / and I work to alter
them and improve them . . . . Against Nature's silence
I use action.

The position of the two characters has thus been
established and the crucial problem has been defined.

Sade's attitude is determined by a kind of passivity. He has examined the Enlightenment doctrine of potential absolute within a pluralistic society. Further—and this is of prime importance—he has lived it through to the end and has been disillusioned; radical egotism is his response. The world of the prison, indifferent and inevitable, cannot be changed and must therefore be reenvisioned as a sensual universe. The cruelty of nature is internalized and perverted into private pleasure-seeking. Introversion versus extraversion; faith in the self versus faith in the "object"—Sade on the one side, and on the other Marat, who defends his belief in the revolution and sees the nature of human institutions rather than human nature as the explanation for the prevailing conditions. His faith is intact, unshakable. Marat is able to preserve his faith by refusing to grasp man anthropologically, to descend into the pit and to interpret him by means of depth psychology. This attitude brings out the tenets of historical materialism. According to Marx, man's existence is not determined by his consciousness; on the contrary, it is his social existence that determines his consciousness. This concept permits Marat to express an "idealistic" point of view, while Sade responds to this historical-sociological view, which foreshadows Marx, with Freudian psychology. As a result the two men, to the extent that they are viewed not as two aspects of a single individual but as two alternatives, must speak past each other. In fact, the dialogue is a monologue for two voices; it does not progress dialectically but sums up positions in declarative statements.

Sade's psychologically based position becomes clear in scene 15, "Continuation of the Conversation between Marat and Sade." If man's thoughts, feelings, and will are mere functions of material data, then ethics—the answer to the question, "How shall we act?"—is superfluous. But man must act; he acts every day, every hour. What do we know of him? Who lies concealed behind his mask—executioner or victim? It is Peter Weiss's familiar

question. Sade therefore says, "Before deciding what is
wrong and what is right / first we must find out what
we are / . . . and the only truths we can point to / are
the ever-changing truths of our own experience / I do
not know if I am hangman or victim." Sade concludes
that "The Revolution / no longer interests me." Turning
toward Marat, he sums up the situation: "You lie in your
bath / . . . alone with your ideas about the world /
which no longer fit the world outside." The discrepancy
between idea and reality is blatantly obvious when Marat's
utopianism is compared with the sorry present.

La Philosophie dans le boudoir ou les Instituteurs
libertins is the title of a work by Sade published in 1795.
Its seven dialogues are accompanied by so-called discussions. In the fifth dialogue the libertine Dolmance expounds his philosophy of absolute liberation of the individual, the total abolition of all binding norms, thereby
assuming a counterposition to the citizens' revolution,
which believed in humanity and in the possibility of
peaceful coexistence. Capital punishment is also rejected,
on the grounds that it is administrative murder, while
murder for the sake of revenge and sexual gratification
are admitted into the new value system based on egotism
and cruelty.

In scene 20 Peter Weiss's Sade has Charlotte Corday
flog him while he delivers his long monologue. Philosophic
credo and sadomasochistic excess are dovetailed. Alluding
to Les Cent-vingt Journées de Sodome, ou l'école du
libertinage (written in 1785), de Sade confesses under
the blows of the whip that he is tortured by self-loathing
and that in his prison cell images had appeared to him of
"monstrous representatives of a dying class" who could
only exercise their power in spectacularly staged orgies.
In enumerating the mechanics of their atrocities in the
minutest detail, he is not so much attacking these drown-
ing persons who are pulling down with them whatever they
are still able to clutch as he is indicting himself. The
recording self must be understood as an eye witness, a

participant, whose self-observation grants him a sympto-
matic picture of his time. "In a criminal society / I dug
the criminal out of myself / so I could understand him
and so understand the times we live in." Initially Sade
saw in the Revolution the chance for a tremendous "out-
burst" of revenge, for an "orgy" greater than all his
dreams. But when he himself sat in the courtroom as a
judge and had the power to deliver the prisoners to the
hangman, he could not do it. He recognizes the gulf that
separates killing as an aesthetic act from killing as a
political act, death in the form of administrative murders,
as we have called it, from personal murder for reasons
of revenge or sexual gratification, which leads to freedom
by arousing the individual.

Peter Weiss's Sade comes to realize two differences
—that between literature and action and that between
the individual and society. He recognizes the conflicts
inherent in the Revolution, which promises liberation but
requires the sacrifices of freedom to make it possible. An
absolute revolution that would encompass body and mind,
the individual as well as the collective, cannot be realized. On the other hand, by recording the monstrosities
of a society to which he is committed and by advocating
murder as a moving force for the individual—though, as
a rational being, he is unable to perform it—Sade creates
a position of intellectual freedom for himself. Though he
is unable either to turn his philosophy into a reality or
to endorse another philosophy, he can speak out. As a
result he is completely thrown back upon himself, into an
emotional isolation analogous to his internment in Charenton. His position is that of the aesthete, the conscious
voyeur, the recorder.

He has realized that the Revolution finally brought
the possibility of revenge and liberation, even in the sense
that, by freeing man, it gave him the possibility to live
to the fullest. But just as the liberation of the masses
means bondage and extinction for the individual, the
release of the collective drive brings chaos and anarchy,

since setting free the lion in man of necessity unleashes
the jackal as well. Total freedom in the collective sense
is impossible. It exists in art, in the subjective, private
world of the individual. Thus we learn the paradoxical
truth that man's absolute liberation in the collective leads
to inhumanity.

The dialogue between Marat and Sade continues in
scene 28. "Give up," Sade coaxes Marat, who has
covered his ears with his hands; nothing can be achieved
by "scribbling." He, too, has long ago abandoned his
masterpiece. All writing vanishes, as does everything
thought and planned. Marat tries to justify himself. When
he wrote, he always wrote with action in mind; he was
perfectly aware that writing was just a preparation. To
Sade, who persists, Marat's proclamations are nothing but
lies. "What do you still want from the revolution /
where is it going / Look at these lost revolutionaries."
Marat cannot refute Sade's arguments. "Everything I
wrote or spoke / was considered and true / each argument was sound / And now I doubt / why does everything sound false." Is he really ahead of his time "by a
century," as the four singers comfortingly claim? Their
concluding sentence rather restricts their meaning: "Your
words have turned into a flood / which covers all France
with her people's blood."

Once more, in scene 30, Sade expounds the opposition of instinct and idea, of body and mind. But he immediately adds that revolution goes with copulation. His
claim, as already stated, is that man's liberation must be
absolute. Not only the world of the mind but the world of
the body as well is awaiting liberation. The Bastille has
taught Sade that this is a world of bodies and that each
body pulses with a terrible power, each one alone and
racked with its own unrest. These cells of the inner self
are worse than the deepest stone dungeon, and as long as
they are locked, all revolutions are only a prison mutiny.
It is the thinking of Freud, the Surrealists, and Henry
Miller that is expressed here. The play would have reached

its climax, the murder, in scene 30 had not the herald
blown "shrilly on his whistle" in order to put an "in-
terruptus" into the "act."

The manner of Charlotte Corday's approach to
Marat with "an expression of hate and lust" reveals the
author's intention—combining pain and sexual thrill, in
Sade's way. The murder is to be seen as the travesty of a
sexual encounter. After it has taken place, the Marquis
stands upright on his chair, laughing triumphantly. Not
silence but laughter concludes the grotesque tale of
horror. The definitive published German version includes
in the epilogue of scene 33 a direct address to the
audience by the herald: "Before you walk out through
the door / let us briefly sum up once more / what we
have tried to say." He then questions Sade about the
play's outcome. Sade replies that he had intended to test
out antitheses and clear up doubts. Though the play has
no definitive ending, he opposes the road taken by Marat.
The present situation still leaves him faced with an
unanswered question.

Are we really dealing with an unanswered question?
True, individualism is opposed to socialism, and Sade's
absolute freedom contrasts with the relative liberation
espoused by Marat. But we must remember that the play
is set in a postrevolutionary society, in which the freedom
demanded by Marat has theoretically become a reality
and that the new society is ruled by egotism, perverted
individualism. This society is headed by an emperor who
both embodies and negates the Revolution. That the idea,
the principle of "not yet," the hope nevertheless remains
alive is revealed by Roux's words which conclude the
play and possibly sum up the author's intention:
"When will you learn to see / when will you learn to take
sides." They refer to the last of the three steps—
postulating the revolution, the impossibility of realizing
it without destroying our image of man; affirming its
necessity. The affirmation of this necessity, however, is
embedded in laughter, which is in turn partly negated by

the fact that Roux is quasi identical with his part, thus
speaking for himself, the political prisoner, as well.

The play is revealed to be a grotesque; it refers to
Mockinpott's solution for universal problems, thus es-
pousing the "third point of view," determined by skepticism, corresponding to that of the four singers and the
harlequin-herald. "I hold the third point of view," Peter
Weiss said in a 1965 interview. "I don't like it myself. . . .
I write in order to find out where I stand, and therefore
I have to introduce all my doubts every time." Subsequently Weiss explained "the easy third point of view"
as the "back door through which I was able to escape into
the no-man's land of pure imagination."

Brecht's *Threepenny Opera* remained open-ended,
offering no definitive solution. But it marked a turning
point—sympathy with anarchy consolidated into radical
political commitment. A similar situation takes place in
Marat/Sade. Self-analysis and social analysis fuse in this
play, which calls for revolution even as it demonstrates
its impossibility. However, the title and the external
events must not be allowed to conceal the fact that it is
not primarily Marat's death that is at stake; rather, the
play stages an intellectual act and its consequences, embedded in contrapuntal, interrelated scenes. Their topic
is the contradictions of the revolution. Sade does not
contradict Marat; both of them together, and Roux with
them, state the opposition to Coulmier and to the so-called
bourgeois society which he represents. It is Sade and the
play versus the lunatic asylum and the audience. Although
Marat and Sade hold the stage, the dialogue between them
is in reality a dialogue of the author with himself. Marat's
thoughts are the author's thoughts, a constitutive element
of a Strindberglike self-analysis.

In other words, put simply, Marat is the embodiment
of Sade's unrealized thoughts, the metaphorical mask of
a possible way of life. The brutal, hypocritical world
which is constantly unmasked by the discrepancy between the ideal of the Revolution as it is conjured up in

the dialogue and the reality, becomes the target of harsh criticism—though it is given an alibi in the overall dramatic structure. Sade and Marat are writers. One records the history of a dying social class—the reference to *The Insurance Policy* is unmistakable—the other carries "his soul" in his "brain." Both want the revolution, with the difference that Sade has seen through its contradictions and confronts "nature" with literature, whereas Marat replies to "Nature's silence" with "action" and hope. He believes in the possibility of a revolution that will radically alter social conditions.

Sade's view of Marat reveals his own past to him. The skeptic examines the idealist he used to be. The reality in which his play is unfolding furnishes constant proof of how well founded his skepticism is. He is the revolutionary who failed at the moment when he recognized the perversion an idea undergoes when it is about to become action. He, the writer who had defended the individual's right to himself, to absolute egotism, to the opening of the "cells of the inner self," is now forced to experience the discrepancy between idea and action. A revolution that raises vagrancy to the level of a social structure and demands total liberation of the individual and the release of instinctual drives of body and mind must drown in anarchy. The opposition of individual and collective without the sacrifice of one or the other can be reconciled completely only in imagination. Aestheticism, the passivity of the voyeur, and literature take the place of the revolution which he must demand as an enlightened witness of the times. The one-sided agitation of Céline is replaced by Henry Miller. Therein lies the significance and the topicality of the play, understood on the basis of the author himself.

The contradiction between literature and politics, aestheticism and action, the tension between mind and instinct, individual and collective, probably the most fruitful topic of discussion today, is expressed by Sade and vividly demonstrated in his fashion—by making the

political murder take place as an aesthetic, perverted
event before an audience. Charlotte Corday's confusion
of the political ideal with sexual satisfaction, of Marat's
murder with her quest for thrills lends the problem an
unusually tangible form. And what about Marat? A fig-
ment of Sade's imagination, a character filled with hate
for his father and his monarch, he acts pragmatically,
controlling the revolution by a combination of spirit and
action. He makes the Revolution relative in order to make
it functional.

Since the self of those who call for liberation consists
of body as well as of mind, but since the complete
emancipation of the body leads to egotism and anarchy,
he suppresses the body for the sake of the soul. Though
he is thus an engineer of the revolution, his reign is also
that of a life-denying functionary. His executions in the
name of the people foreshadow the efficient lethal
machinery active in the concentration camps and else-
where. His "abstract" relationship to "life" places him
in opposition to the revolution just as much as Sade
because of *his* position. If, on the other hand, freedom
can be realized only if man is willing to restrict it according to ethical considerations, but if the idea of the collective is defined precisely by the collective incapacity of
such a restriction, another contradiction arises which
further complicates the problem. What remains is a conflict inherent in any revolution, political or artistic.

The undiminished importance of *Marat/Sade* rests
precisely in the fact that this personal testimony—an internal monologue translated into theater—lays bare a
basic phenomenon of human existence: the irreconcilable
tension between the natural psychophysical character
of man and the claims of an inevitable idea that has been
objectively and ideologically acknowledged. Seen from
this angle, the problem posed by the play may recall the
thirteen books of Augustine's *Confessions*, to risk a far-
fetched comparison. Tormented and molded by sensitivity,
sensuality, and a passion for knowledge, Augustine found

in Christianity the salvation for an all-encompassing, reconciling "truth." The path of the maturing Peter Weiss is marked by a similar influence. As we shall see, it leads to a highly problematic form of theater which is in itself contradictory.

It is tempting to link Peter Weiss's reaction to the conflicts exposed in *Marat/Sade* with Tertullian's famous "credo quia absurdum." Also appropriate here is Martin Esslin's statement (in *The Theatre of the Absurd*) that the irrational Theatre of the Absurd and the highly purposeful politically committed play are not so much irreconcilable contradictions, as rather, the obverse and reverse side of the same medal. Marxism also reconciles the contradiction inherent in the concept of freedom at the same time that it rejects psychoanalysis as a blurring view of the true social conditions. To the Marxist, freedom remains a fiction—as in the final analysis it does for Sade —since man's thoughts and actions are in actuality determined by instinct and environment. According to this eschatological line of thought, the debate between Marat and Sade about freedom may consequently be considered irrelevant and outdated. Discussions of economics and the class struggle take its place.

The dualism of Sade and Marat, revealed as a conundrum, parallels the contradiction that shattered Expressionism and ultimately caused the waning of Surrealism. The drama of Marat and Sade is also the drama of the inner contradiction of Surrealism, which strove for the reconciliation of life and art, thought and action, individual and collective. Absolute freedom and absurd action on the one hand and the Marxist demand for harmony and happiness of the greatest number of people on the other, account for the discrepancy which blew up the Surrealists. Peter Weiss became deeply concerned with the movement and its history. Sade is notoriously considered the "ancestor" and "quintessential image of Surrealist man." Breton repeatedly refers to Sade's striving for moral and social liberation; he praises his heroic

struggle to create a new order of things and defines his
"own path" as leading through Sade. Surrealism opposes
rote drill, utility, traditional morality, submission, practical activity, realism, to name only a few points of
attack. The slogan of the liberation of man is one of its
recurring theses. The road leads inward, into the fastnesses
of the self, to observation of whatever takes place in the
depth of man—it leads to self-analysis. Interest is focused
on the subconscious, the miraculous, dreams, madness,
hallucinatory states—in other words everything outside
the rational, or pure life. Surrealism bases itself on Freud
as having made it possible for man to enjoy his essential
possession, freedom.

The attack on society is linked with the demand for
the liberation of love. Freud's interpretation of the libido
as the main incentive to action and conduct implies an
accusation of concealment and hypocrisy imposed by the
standards of society. Every man has to have the right to
satisfy his omnipotent desires, as Sade already claimed.
The ideal of the Surrealists is "total" revolution. It means
not only a change in the social order, but also the abolition of the restrictive conditions of human existence, an
opening to urges and desires.

Initially the Surrealist revolution aimed at mobi-
lizing the thinking of all mankind: Henry Miller's concepts
follow a similar line. According to Raymond Queneau
(cited in Maurice Nadeau, *Histoire du Surrealisme*, Paris
1945), it is a change of "the innermost essence of man
. . . of the thought process." However, there was more
than merely idealism, a revolution of the mind. It was
amplified by the idea of revolutionizing social conditions by an alliance with the Communist Party and the
transition toward dialectical materialism. Any representative of the movement, they declared, must take the only
revolutionary road, the road of Marxism; he must—in
Nadeau's words—"jump the ditch . . . which separates
absolute idealism from dialectical materialism." Study of
and experimenting with the inner life of the individual

was to be continued, but so was social revolution and collective action.

How can the dogma of "unconditional indignation, total insubordination, opposition, and systematic sabotage" (as André Breton put it in his *Manifestoes of Surrealism*) be reconciled with the readiness to form a "united front" with the Communist Party? At the time of the war in Morocco, Breton expressed the opinion that under present conditions true art must side with social revolutionary activity; like the latter, it strives to bring confusion into the capitalist social order and to prepare its downfall.

As long as it had only been a question of the revolution as such, there had been only minimal "dissention," Nadeau noted. Emerging factions within the Surrealist movement had argued whether or not Surrealism was the same as the revolution. After 1930 Surrealism continued on two parallel tracks—the political revolution and exploration of the subconscious, liberating of the life within. We feel reminded of the juxtaposition of Marat and Sade, who may be said to correspond to Aragon and Dali within the camp of the Surrealists. We know, after all, that the movement eventually split into two directions, art and revolution.

Revolutionary individualism on the one side, and revolutionary change of environment and society on the other would together result in the "total revolution" in which surrealists would be Marxists as well as Freudians. Understandably the Surrealists tried to salvage the "idea" of the revolution, which the Soviet regime had perverted, by identifying with Trotsky, who had been expatriated and expelled from the Soviet Union in 1929. In the "Second Surrealist Manifesto," published in 1930, Breton claims that the revolutionary principles of poetic determinism and dialectic materialism are "exactly alike," even though, or precisely because, a proletarian culture has not yet been realized. He quotes extensively from Trotsky's *Literature and Revolution* and extends the

future, which had been considered as having begun, into
the realm of faith in the fulfillment which is sure to come.
In Trotsky's view, the evolution of the new social order
would certainly bring the day when economics, culture,
and art would enjoy the greatest freedom of movement
(that of progress). Only assumptions on that subject
were possible, however, assumptions based on imagination. Trotsky wrote these optimistic words half a century
ago. One of Peter Weiss's latest plays is called *Trotsky
in Exile*. Its eponymous hero states that failures and disappointments cannot stop him from seeing beyond the
present defeat to a rising of the oppressed everywhere.
This, claims Trotsky, is no utopian prophecy, but the
"sober prediction" of dialectical materialism. Breton
concluded his argument with the belief that man would
be wrong to despair because of a few monstrous historical
defeats. He retains the freedom of believing in his freedom. Belief and faith can close the chasm revealed in the
conversation between Marat and Sade and unbridgeable
by Surrealism.

Marat/Sade, essentially a play of ideas, is a dramatic
montage structured on three levels, with contrasting
effects. Its inner unity, not unlike the mystery play, is
based on the unchanging ego identity of the hero or the
author, who experiences his own (subjective) past as an
alien (objective) present. The external unity of its
"open" structure is founded on the nature of the grotesque
tabloid ballad. The outline and basic attitude of this play
about a play and its performance are epic. The author,
or in his stead the characters representing him—the four
singers and the herald—present the show. The titles given
each scene are like arguments. They include "Corday
Is Introduced," "Corday's First Visit," and "Sade Turns
His Back on All the Nations." The epic title of the play
is in itself tendentious. This technique is as reminiscent
of the *commedia dell'arte*, which the character of the
herald recalls in particular, as of epic theater. To put it
simply, the play represents an "epic for two voices" in

which two theses confront each other without ever achieving dialogue. Because the contrast between the two central characters is maintained to the end, the play may be defined as based on a "static split." The schism reflects the "third point of view" of the author, the "unanswered question."

The structural principle of *Marat/Sade* is association, connecting the various skits. This technique of appositive conjunction furthers the action, Sade being its dramatic center, embodied on stage as author and spectator.

Its qualities of grotesque tabloid ballad and cabaret place the play in the category of works between epic and drama which held the stage toward the end of the first quarter of the twentieth century. Its montage is composed of elements of the side show, theater of cruelty, and if the term can be allowed, philosophical conversation piece.

It is debatable whether the historico-political subject is thus given adequate expression or whether the exuberance of the theatrical means forces it toward neutralization and dissolution in irrationality and phantasmagoria. In this respect the play differs radically from Brecht's intentions. In Brecht's theater the stage effects are extremely economical and strictly differentiated. The activating impulse is aimed at reason, deliberately downplaying feelings and emotions. Although both fall back on extraliterary impulses of expression, and though *Marat/Sade* is epic theater, the traits of "culinary" theater, justified by Sade's fictitious authorship, are dominant. While the montage of a multiplicity of actions, props, and language levels successfully produces an alienation effect, it also creates an atmosphere of illusion which smothers the didactic purpose. *Marat/Sade* is "total" theater, "all-encompassing spectacle" in the sense of "theater of cruelty." According to Artaud, even while sensibility must be stimulated and ecstasy increased to the point of "paroxysm," the author must strive to heighten the significance of every spoken word. These contrasts correspond to those of body and mind, of the release of the instincts versus reflection. This complex purpose is served by the mobilization of all the means of expression that can be used on stage, such as music, pantomime, and gestures, as Artaud noted in his essay "Staging and Metaphysics."

Peter Weiss has added songs, and given the herald complete madrigals to speak. Nevertheless, the methods of "Theater of Cruelty" preponderate, and especially by frequent use of pantomime they produce the very multiplying effect that foreshadows documentary theater. At the end of the play the patients march forward in blind excitement, screaming, "Copulation Copulation." The frenzied column comes close to the audience. It is almost as though stage and spectators might fuse, in keeping with Artaud's romantic, ironic hope for his Theater of Cruelty.

Marat/Sade marked a climax as well as a turning point in the work of Peter Weiss. It is both a sober backward look and a summing up. A force field stretches between the opposing positions of Sade and Coulmier, of Freudianism and the repressive power of the state; this was crucially important in the author's development, as has been shown by our examination of the works that preceded *Marat/Sade*. Sade, the victim of established morality, of the moral code of a society characterized by neuroses and repressed aggression, confronts Coulmier, the guardian of the restorative middle class.

Examination of the themes and subjects of the earlier works, especially the autobiographical writings, proves that Peter Weiss's development and self-discovery occurred in dialogues with certain authoritative individuals. His choice of Kafka, Hesse, Miller, and finally Sade as thematic correspondents to his view of life, and of Strindberg and Artaud as figures who parallel his aesthetic and formalistic attitudes indicates the interior journey the author has now completed. Later, Trotsky, in the political sphere, joins their number.

Guides and Analogues

The man who was to write *Marat/Sade* found a reflection of his own emotional state in Kafka's work. It is determined by a feeling of exclusion, of standing outside a sealed-off world. The consciousness of the impossibility of freedom, of the inevitability of an unfathomable world, led Peter Weiss into inwardness, without clarifying the escape. Kafka's vision of freedom and his utopian notion of man's responsibility for himself remain nebulous in Weiss. His road to inwardness is fraught with nightmares, images of menace and danger, where environment, family, school, and society are paralyzingly present. Freedom remains a pipe dream, since reality is not his reality but that of the others—it is hell. Weiss claims that only once during his childhood did he feel an intimation of physical freedom. Self-analysis took its place, of the sort that fills Harry Haller's notes in Hesse's *Steppenwolf*. Isolation and disgust with the world constitute Haller's vision of the absolute and the situation of middle-class infantile inexperience, the incapacity to integrate naked animalism into his own existence. It is the rebellion of his own nature against a society ruled by frustration. Anxiety becomes somehow thrilling, it serves as a substitute for the vitality that had been frustrated because the person was not in harmony with the attitudes and manifestations of the "obligatory image" of man. The feelings of anxiety and menace, the flight to inwardness, were joined by an awareness of guilt. The conviction

eventually crystallized that his own problems were due
to a life-denying ethos. Middle-class morality, which
demanded submission to violence rather than the exercise
of violence, turns its adherents into accomplices whenever
barbarism triumphs.

In this connection Hesse's continued influence, especially in America, may be explained by the fact that
he creates the illusion of limited freedom for the young
contemporary who is exposed to the exaggerated pressure
of a bureaucratic, repressive society. He confronts the
civilized world with the inner world—a force field where
good and evil are considered to have equal power to de-
termine destiny, as in Chinese cosmology. This view opens
up the possibility of an apparently limitless unfolding
of the personality. Become who you are, is the exhortation
at the end of Nietzsche's definition of being as becoming
and of his concept of *amor fati*. The union with destiny
of Hesse becomes a union with creation in Miller.

Kafka is the star witness of futility, the representative of what Peter Weiss has called "the twisted guilt-laden
doomed and damned bourgeoisie" (though this amounts
to a misunderstanding of the fundamental, ontological
nature of his work); Hesse is the writer who disclosed
the abysses of the self, who leads the reader to see the
wolf next to the lamb, and who promises freedom; and
finally, there is Henry Miller, the liberator. He tells the
whole truth, as no one has told it since the *Confessions*
of Jean-Jacques Rousseau. The world is "terrifying,"
Miller claims, but it is "good." As in Hesse's case, commitment to it must include everything, even what is called
evil and base. It is a crime not to live life fully. Civilization is opposed to the cosmic bond. The protest against
the world of civilization takes place in the delivery, in
the release of the ego drive, in the sexual act. The return
to nature is transformed into a return to sexuality. Sexual
activity is considered a cure for the ills of civilization. It
is obvious that Miller's "shock of obscenity" is of use
neither to the marketplace nor to the collective. It is the

experience of the outsiders. The individual can therefore achieve freedom only by the individual act which leads back to the sources, to the archaic. In other words, Miller's erotic hypothesis cannot become a realized liberating action in the shape of a universally ameliorating law, any more than can Sade's vision. There is the difference, however, that Miller detached himself from the "buffalo herd" and avoids it, whereas Sade tried to bridge the gap by participating in the revolution. Miller remains in the realm of art to which Sade, resigned, returned. Miller's art—his aesthetic program, if we wish to call it that—refers back to Surrealism, with its release of the hidden creative forces—dream, intoxication, and image.

In a lecture promisingly titled "Gegen die Gesetze der Norm" (Against the Laws of the Norm) Peter Weiss noted that when he was fifteen or sixteen he was drawn to the writings of the "anarchic" Strindberg. The extent of the visions of this revolutionary can be grasped in full only today, Weiss claimed. Strindberg had the courage to express the inner conflict—to reveal himself in his contradictions. He drew up the project for a new and timely theater. Characters in the traditional sense were to Strindberg merely signs of conformity which stifled the revolution. His need to fragment characters found its expression in his choice of a "collage technique" which is still valid for the modern theater, according to Peter Weiss. The character on whom Strindberg focused his main interest was Strindberg himself. He made himself into an object of investigation, of vivisection; he portrayed his advance in uncharted territory and opened up possibilities for new forms of expression.

What does writing mean to him? He tells us in *A Dream Play*: "Not reality—more than reality. Not a dream—but conscious dreaming." The concepts of self-analysis and dream again refer to expressionism and surrealism. The importance of vision and dream into which the action dissolves, the division of the main figure into "aspects," into embodiments of its various possibilities, have been noted many times. Strindberg was a pioneer. The beggar in *To Damascus*, the first expressionist drama, is a facet of the leading character embodying his repressed and unrealized feelings and thoughts. He is given the function of a leitmotif, as it were. This device is one of the sources of Peter Weiss's method of splitting his characters, as seen in *The Tower* and especially in *Marat/Sade*.

His encounter with the practice and theories of Surrealism were without question of outstanding importance for Peter Weiss. His remarks indicate that the great forerunners—Lautréamont, Jarry, Apollinaire, Artaud, Breton, and others—became his guides and analogues. The connection between Surrealism and Dante, Sade, Strindberg, Freud, and Miller has been established. Directly or indirectly each of them constituted a provocation or a confirmation that led to confrontation; there were Dante's, Sade's, and Sartre's experiences of "hell" as well as Freud's and Miller's roads to liberation. Lautréamont is the author to whom the Surrealists refer most often. They struggle to create works that will equal his. According to Nadeau, no one stimulated and nourished Surrealism as much as Lautréamont, especially by his liberation of man's "will," which plays a dominant role also in the writings of Schopenhauer and Nietzsche—a liberation in writing, in literature. The work of Peter Weiss also shows traces of an interest in Lautréamont. Like Sade, Lautréamont—another forerunner of Freud— wanted to uncover the snake pit that was so zealously kept covered by religion and morality. The image of darkness awakens a yearning for light. Is this apocalyptic vision allied to Hieronymus Bosch and the "hellish Breughel," a tradition shared by Lautréamont? Peter Weiss also describes hell, the "inferno."

Weiss's affinity particularly with Artaud and the "Theater of Cruelty" has already been pointed out. "Violence and blood" are to be placed at the service of the "power of the mind." Artaud wanted his theater to "reflect, if only on a philosophical plane." These are two of the most important elements which characterize the Marat portion of the play, while at the same time referring to Sade.

Experimental filmmakers, painters, and writers are still at the starting gate, Peter Weiss noted in his essay on films. They must continue to develop; there is again a need for forcible aesthetic action in our "sated, satisfied somnolence." Such violent actions and psychic shock effects are characteristic of Artaud's Theater of Cruelty; they are also present in *Marat/Sade*. More than that, it can be said that *Marat/Sade* is the realization of the legacy left by the great theoretician Artaud.

Antonin Artaud belonged to the second wave of Surrealists. In his essay on film Weiss mentioned him several times. The themes of shock, of rebellion "against the powers of morality," and of sadomasochistic obsessions—especially in the autobiographical writings—apply to Artaud as well as to the avant-garde film and to Surrealism in general. The Surrealist playwright and theoretician of theater tried to transfer the ideas and theses of Surrealism to the stage in his Theater of Cruelty." The theater's function, in his view, is to portray our inhibitions and to resolve them. Cruelty was seen as an expression of menace and a hunger for life. Here, too, the conflict between the individual and society is unavoidable, because Marat's and Sade's positions cannot be reconciled.

It is not surprising that Artaud had also planned to stage one of Sade's tales "in which the erotic would be transposed allegorically, and symbolized; it would be shown as a violent expression of cruelty, while veiling everything else."

On the Possibility of Demonstrating "Objective Absurdity": Pertaining to the Question of "Documentary Theater"

Sade's dialogue with his own past, as objectified in Marat, is characterized by skepticism. But his justification for abandoning hope in the Revolution is itself a rebellious act. For the inmate of a political penitentiary uses his plays to protest against restriction and oppression, against the reality in which his metaphors have become reality, since it is revealed as "objective absurdity." Its perversion is an undeniable fact, although not to the extent to which it became a fact in the twentieth century.

In *Les Cent-vingt Journées de Sodome* the historical Sade has the psychopathic duke insistently warn the forty-two women and boys who are held captive in his castle, "Think about what you are and what we are. . . . You have been taken away from your friends, from your parents. You are dead to the world." The world of terror and the detention camps Sade described, his "catalogue of sex murders" must have sounded as fantastic two hundred years ago as the technical world of the novels of Jules Verne sounded a century later. Those were different times. The means and the goal postulated another fifty years later by the "Theater of Cruelty" must of necessity seem inadequate when the material of reality itself has become so unfathomable, incredible, and absurd that it surpasses all imagination.

Artaud strove to explode a sediment of hidden cruelty which was to bring about purification and catharsis. Though his goal was liberation in the form of allegorical illustrations, he did not see his theater as faced with the competition of a superior evil in human reality. If the theater wishes to take up that challenge, it must combine evocation with information; it must report historical absurdity, which can be analyzed and demonstrated to a certain degree, it must turn to documentary theater. It proceeeds socratically, encouraging change without the need for ideological rigidity. This may correspond to André Breton's definition in 1935 of the two essential components of the revolutionary spirit—one, the refusal to accept the conditions imposed on man accompanied by the urge to change them and, second, absolute loyalty to the moral principles and claims that have allowed the world to progress.

Weiss was not content with these principles. The self-confrontation in *Marat/Sade* was followed by the Auschwitz trial held in Frankfurt. He thought that an explanation for the (objective) absurdity articulated at the trial could be found only in the clichés of dialectical materialism. Passing over the possibilities of documentary theater, he began to write works of political didacticism and pamphlets. Nevertheless, *The Investigation*, the play written in 1964–1965 and following *Marat/Sade*, is considered documentary theater. It is intended as an illustration of the program set forth in his article "Material and Models. Notes toward the Documentary Theater." He claims that the work abstains from invention of any kind; that its authentic materials are presented on the stage unchanged as to content, though given new form. The author's note to the play states, "This condensation should contain nothing but facts." It is a "recording" of reality, this time not based on sober observation as in *The Shadow*, but on documents; it is theater of documentation.

The influence of axiomatic deductive thinking is on the increase. Even the humanities have begun to use methods of logistics and information theory. For literature, this means that the Archimedean position of the self —whose fixity remains, and must remain, the point of departure, although its leverage has become doubtful—is challenged by a reality grounded both in society and in our understanding of technology and the natural sciences. This agrees with Nicolai Hartmann's demonstration of the phenomena as the precondition for intellectual activity. Since a document contains a high degree of objectivity to the extent that it is authentic, its reproduction on stage produces a reality composed of ready-made parts supplied by the subject itself. Theater of documentation relies on nothing but reality for the reproduction of reality; in this way it reduces the cognitive problems, while aesthetic problems are somewhat increased. It challenges the author to combine didactic demonstration with art. On the other hand, the supposedly responsible audience is offered a type of theater which conveys a loose, repeatable experience as a point of view and refrains from drawing conclusions about the subject matter in an effort to present a "truth" that is not linked to any authority, except perhaps to the authority of a moral which has been experienced as an axiom.

Erwin Piscator's response to the admitted inadequacy of the naturalistic theater to portray social conditions was his new format of "political extravaganza." By using new stage techniques to reintroduce the social reality that had had to be excluded, he was able to show the human being as conditioned by economics and politics and to show society, social conditions, as the consequence of both.

Piscator demanded that the material be scientifically analyzed, related to the real world, and thereby turned into "proof." This was possible only, Piscator wrote in *Das politische Theater (Political Theater)* by overcoming the exclusively individualistic aspect of the characters and the chance nature of fate—by creating a link between the stage action and the larger forces of history. Piscator used film as the means of bracketing the stage and life, since it allowed him to insert the data of politics, economics, culture, and society, of sports and fashion, into

the stage action. Saturating the plot with historical facts
revealed that the individual life was conditioned by
society; it objectified and multiplied it. This is not to
overlook the fact that the structure imposed on the events
was determined by an epic I, who causes the whole to
appear as cabaret.

That Bertolt Brecht owes much to this method is
well known. Thus the concept of "documentary theater"
used in this sense can be found in Brecht's writings as
early as 1927. It is obvious, on the other hand, that
Piscator's scientific analysis of the material is only a step
away from radical objectification and total dismissal of
the "fictional" hero. The technical devices for recreating
a courtroom and the opposing sides of a trial, for instance
—magnetic tape, film, and the like—supply the condition
for total history. It becomes clear, however, that not all
materials are suited to "documentation"; not every author
is a born "documentator"; and not every political persuasion yields a suitable point of view.

What is a document and what is documentation?
Since the concept has been used a number of times, it
calls for elucidation. The word "document" comes from
the Latin word for "proof." Modern languages have ex-
tended the meaning to include the sense of legal record.
To document, then, means to prove, to show objectively.
The document presents a reality; it is considered the con-
stituting element of reality, infallible proof that can at
all times be called upon to refute nonreality (untruth).
"Documentation" means the assembling, classification,
and utilization of documents—that is, of all matter that
promotes analysis, information, and the supply of proof,
such as newspapers, letters, files, official records, films,
tapes, and models. Documentation is of particular importance for the judicial and legislative processes, for the
natural sciences, for medicine, for technology, and for
economics. Documentation and argumentation belong together. One makes the other possible, material proof
underlying intellectual proof. The argument supports our

certainty, it serves as its basis; together with the document it creates the foundation in which reality is rooted.
Theater of documentation—or "documentary theater," as
Peter Weiss calls it—is theater based on documents,
theater for which there exists "official proof." If the
concept is interpreted according to its meaning, it reveals
its reality based on the document.

While documentation is proof by registration, the
argumentation intended to assist it requires rationality,
the availability of reason and belief in reason. This is the
idea Diderot had in mind when he demanded that men
be led to truth by reason, not by violence. Conversely, it
is pointless to discuss what happens to a documentation
when its complement, rationality, severs itself from the
ethical humanitarian ideals which are an element in its
definition. In other words, we arrive at the paradoxical
situation that documentation retains its ability to reflect
reality and remains material proof only as long as critical
rationality, which is largely objective and value-free, is
used to deal with it.

As mentioned, theater of documentation belongs to
the tradition of the Enlightenment; it aims at ending what
Kant has called self-inflicted tutelage. The reference is
more than ever relevant. It excludes attitudes based on
religious and political authority. It sets a higher value on
the quest for truth than on a truth bound to authority or
authenticated or prescribed by it. The same holds true for
theater of documentation, which exaggerates its own purpose the moment it dispenses with argumentation, rationality, and the willingness to make revisions—that is, as
soon as it forgets to subject its own position to critical
reflection. Causal and functional analyses are meant to
further heightened understanding. The stage activity is
paralleled by a possibly contrary process in the consciousness of the spectator.

No one will deny that such a turning toward the
persuasive powers of rational argumentation, toward the
enlightening effect of constructive imagination, can stimu-

late literature to new efforts, particularly at a time when there is increased sensitivity to any form of persuasion or propaganda and when, surprisingly, demythification has been succeeded by a wave of unmistakable remythification. On the other hand, the weaknesses of theater of documentation are obvious, especially because it addresses itself so unmistakably to the "critical rationality" of the spectator. This theater, too, is a form of fiction—that is, a form of literature.

The "weak point" of theater of documentation lies in its "intent." As a product of artistic techniques—the documentary material must be structured for the stage— it not only "is" reality, it also "intends" to be reality. It is, for good or ill, also a nonreality, a symbol, and as such it is more than, and different from, "is."

Even if in contrast to a purely fictional work of art, a writer employs larger blocks of reality for his edifice— blocks that still show traces of being close to the source, so to speak—even if he adopts the material with hardly any changes, the dramatic concept according to which he constructs his work is nonetheless derived from his "intent." The emphasis on the "material" (which, together with the author's intent, supplies the "symbolic structure" of art) to the detriment of the "intent" must not veil the fact that the documented trial is not the trial itself and that the material is changed in one way or another by the operation of the conceptualizing intention. The role of the author becomes all the more important because it is his attitude that determines the preservation of the values of documentation and of argumentation. As the explaining and enlightening person, he must remember at all times that he is walking a tightrope; otherwise he runs the danger of undermining his own effort.

The objectivity inherent in the concept of documentation is negated and makes nonsense of the purpose of documentation to the extent that the author, who is striving to achieve stage reality, no longer serves the material but makes use of the material and deprives it of autonomy. When a court case becomes a show trial, the spectator is not enlightened; he is subjected to propaganda, he is reduced.

As demonstrated by such plays as Heinar Kipphardt's *In der Sache J. Robert Oppenheimer* (tr. *In the Matter of J. Robert Oppenheimer*), documentary theater can be Socratic. The almost exclusive use of documentary material unreworked though adapted to stage requirements—to provide a clarifying and critical view—is a dialectical road to opinion formation. Since the author is intent on illuminating condition and therefore needs to mobilize reason, he creates a tension between the moral standards on stage (which are to be corrected) and the judgment of the audience. The confusion resulting from the discrepancy leads to reflection and commitment. The audience has the last word, the function of the author has become the Socratic guide.

After *Marat/Sade*, all Peter Weiss's work concentrated on "documentation." Sade had still been able to stage Marat's end as culinary theater, the murder as love play, confirming the writer's position as voyeur; but in the subsequent plays individualism, which Sade opposed to Marat's concept of the collective, has been altogether retired. These plays reveal a changed Peter Weiss, who declares that action and effects are his aims, which he tries to achieve by "documentary theater." It may be asked whether it is possible to achieve a documentary theater that can claim to be a "theater of documentation" such as Kipphardt has brought about while satisfying the goals Peter Weiss has set for his "documentary theater."

In "Material and Models," written in 1968, he claims that documentary theater rejects all forms of invention, that it uses authentic materials, reproducing them on stage with their content unchanged though formally restructured. Such a theater is directed to criticism of concealment, of falsifications of reality, and of lies; it opposes anyone commited to a politics that obscures and blinds.

The essay goes on to note that the strength of the documentary theater lies in its capacity to assemble a usable sample, a model, of actual events from fragments of reality while taking the position of the observer and the analyst. Documentary theater is not interested in arousing emotional involvement; rather, it is intent on presenting facts so that they can be examined. The various parties confront each other; a trial, a court action is described and analytically reproduced. The purpose is to reveal its "exemplary" aspect.

Up to this point the prospectus may be summed up by the concepts of "explanation" and "information." But the second part amends the first and makes these general observations as a whole seem tailored exclusively to fit Peter Weiss's own plays. In Weiss's view, documentary theater must be "partisan" in the sense of the term used by Lenin and Lukács; it forgoes objectivity; its goal is to explain reality in every detail and make it plausible, impenetrable though it may be. In conclusion the essay claims that documentary theater is opposed to the type of playwrighting that "is mainly preoccupied with its own rage and desperation" and that stubbornly clings to the concept of an "absurd and inevitable world."

Instead of illuminating this inevitability, which is dismissed as the ideology of the "inexplicable," documentary theater equates the "understood" world with reality. The document is placed at the service of explicability, which endows it with an ideologically defined reality.

There is no need to dwell at length on the contradiction inherent in such a program. It nullifies the concept of documentary theater as it must be understood if it is to have any meaning. An impressive example of the practical application of Peter Weiss's theory is his *Song of the Lusitanian Bogey*. We will return to the problem of documentary theater in our discussion of that work.

Making the World Aware of the (Capitalist) Inferno as the Condition for the (Socialist) Paradiso: *The Investigation*

Auschwitz was a place for which he had been destined but which he escaped, Peter Weiss said in 1964, the same year in which he began working on *Die Ermittlung* (tr. *The Investigation*), an oratorio in eleven cantos. Biographical concern is one of the key motives for Peter Weiss's interest in the subject of Auschwitz, the symbol of hell on earth. Emotion and vision are here given a concrete and tangible shape. As early as the period 1960–1961, in a backward look at his own past, Peter Weiss, who was always conscious of the fact that survival was bound up with a feeling of guilt, spoke to this point in *Vanishing Point*, on the occasion of first seeing one of the documentaries that showed the full extent of the murders committed in the shadow of the swastika. Two questions arise—the historical one, about how such a thing could possibly have happened, and the human question, about man's psychic and spiritual makeup that makes him capable of such deeds. It is a psychological as well as a political and social problem, and Marxism offers a way to solve it.

The world as inferno—this slogan recalls Dante. In fact, in 1965 Peter Weiss studied the *Divina commedia*. The division of *Mockinpott* into eleven scenes and that of *Marat/Sade* into thirty-three, in an analogy with the thirty-three cantos each of the *Inferno*, the *Purgatorio*, and the *Paradiso*, are evidence of Peter Weiss's interest.

His concern with Dante is further reflected in the short works "Vorübung zum dreiteiligen Drama *divina commedia* ("Preliminary Exercise for the Tripartite Drama, the *Divina commedia*") and in "Gespräch über Dante" ("Discourse on Dante").

First of all, what is the purpose of a "preliminary exercise"? The author's thoughts turn on the difference between Giotto and Dante. Another opposition is seen in the fact that Giotto's world is "tangible nature," including the passions, while Dante's world is detached and marked by the pain of reflection. The author's thoughts about the longer work—which was never written—are reminiscent of Sade's dialogue with Marat; they encompass the present and the past, comparing the two, each reflecting the other. Is it possible to wash away the guilt? Is there still the possibility of "purification" as Dante knew it? The modern writer who questions justice and suffering on earth sees himself at a disadvantage by comparison with Dante. Dante's world was comprehensible, it was "intact" and "whole"; today's poet, on the other hand, is faced with "formlessness," does not have a full perspective on his material, which can no longer be simplified. Things that still held true for Giotto and Dante and could be expressed as visions can no longer be presented as "imagination." Reality has caught up with the vision of hell. Instead of "destroyers" or "good men," who were as tangible as the measure of their punishment or their reward, the modern world offers only nameless persons on both sides, nothing but the survivors of a universal "devaluation."

Peter Weiss wrote this sketch during or after his work on *The Investigation* (1964–1965). This work uses Auschwitz as the subject for "world theater" on the one hand and for a drama of documentation on the other. Unless, that is, the play of documentation itself contains elements of world theater, with tangible parts because they are imposed, a "theocentric parable" (E. R. Curtius) without a God. It stands as a secularized world court, passing judgment on roles defined by a dramatic structure rooted in social conditions.

The Investigation deals not with what happened at Auschwitz, but with the trial as recorded in documents, files, records, tables, figures, and film. In the early summer of 1964 Peter Weiss sat in on the Frankfurt trials. In his search for an answer to his questions, he had visited the remnants of Auschwitz and Birkenau. "Meine Ortschaft" (tr. "My Locality") is the title of his 1964 report.

Auschwitz remains a constant possibility; its psychic potential is within us, the historical fact is all around us. Is it an inherent part of man, of his potential for sinning? Or is it created by the society in which he lives? The answer to these questions can be read in the author's subsequent direction. He found the solution in which an intact world seems again possible. Even before the performance of *The Investigation*, in 1965, Peter Weiss confessed in "10 Arbeitspunkte eines Autors in der geteilten Welt" ("Ten Working Points of an Author in the Divided World") that, given the two electoral choices open to him, he saw only a socialist order as capable of abolishing "the existing ills of world conditions." The final thesis of the essay claims that Weiss has spent most of his working time as well as most of his private life freeing himself "from the narrowness, prejudices, and egotism" imposed upon him by his society; again this indicates that he is elevating private experience to the universal plane.

Of course the material of the trial had of necessity to be condensed and stylized. The reduced number of characters is reflected in heightened speech. The cast is made up of the Judge, the Prosecuting Attorney, Counsel for the Defense, eighteen Accused Persons, and nine Witnesses. Thus the play presents eighteen of the twenty-three accused and nine out of four hundred witnesses.

The characters, then, represent a numerical proportion of three members of the court, nine witnesses, and eighteen accused. The predominance of the number three, a traditional symbol, again makes an allusion to Dante. The titles of the eleven "songs," each of which is also divided into three parts, serve as arguments. They sum up the content and stress the intention of consciousness raising. The titles show the author following the stations of the victims, from their arrival at the platform to the burning of the corpses. He describes the procedure of dehumanization, of dying and of living in abasement, of the reduction to primitive creature existence, which has its own laws and survival as its only goal.

Boger's "swing," the clubs and bullwhips, all belong to the arsenal of instruments of torture that give life and emphasis to obsessions in the work of Peter Weiss. The description of Boger's diabolical activity forms a parallel to Damiens' execution in *Marat/Sade*. Torture, slaughter of every kind—they are terror and mass murder. However, the "investigation" in the concrete "matter" of Auschwitz goes beyond the inventory of the causes for extermination and intimidation—of which Weiss himself had been a potential victim—to the question of destiny and identity which had already been posed in *Vanishing Point*.

Action for change can relieve individual feelings of guilt, especially if the evil is seen on a universal scale, resolving the contradictions between personal existence and the givens of bourgeois society. We listen to Marat accusing Sade of passivity and aestheticism—which the "revolutionary" Nguyen Tuan overcomes in *Vietnam-Notizen (Notes from Vietnam)*—reproaching him indirectly for his lack of action which aligns him "more closely with the murderers and the executioners." The common solution of the problem is reliance on anthropology and psychology, since they explain the question of guilt and innocence as the result of certain life situations, thus both answering and disposing of the questions, as it were. The fault is placed on society, bourgeois society. Changing the one changes the other.

This almost sympathetic, humane attitude toward the executioners contrasts sharply with the condemnation of a society that tolerated the monstrosities and awakened the executioner in man (and in the victim). Being cut off from his own past, Weiss gained a point of view that equates the exploitation and dehumanization of the victims in *The Investigation* with that in the play about Marat and interprets it ideologically. The transition from psychology to politics leads to the subsequent identification almost of the whole Western World with Nazi Germany. At this point, however, the ideology demands that the blame be placed, not so much in the "regime" as on the society that produced it. Solidarity and ideology are considered countermeasures, not only against the possibility of "dehumanization," but also against the capacity to be an "executioner." For this reason the analysis set forth in this play serves more than evidence and accusation; it is a call to rebellion, and thereby the logical continuation of the dialogue begun in *Leavetaking*, *Vanishing Point*, and *Marat/Sade*.

The structure of the play of documentation forces the author to reduce the use of symbolism and to adapt his material to the requirements of the stage at the same time that he furnishes an "interpretation" of the historical material at the expense of its "essence." Objectivity arises from the fact that the play is based not on documentation of the "unfathomable" phenomenon of Auschwitz, but on evidence made "concrete" by the Auschwitz trial. The fact takes on particular significance, since the objectivity of the play of documentation is grounded in these documents —that is, in their accessibility.

In the case of *The Investigation*, documentary theater could have been realized almost to perfection. However, such a realization is hampered both by the external "oratorio" form—with its songs, free verse, and arty ornamentation—and by the conclusion, which is anything but conclusive and clarifying and devaluates the impact of the performed trial, which speaks for itself, by an attempt at propaganda aimed at indicating a cure. The author stands to compromise his credibility as time and again he links the monumental event that provoked the investigation with his own biographical involvement even as he defends a system that confines its unpopular writers in mental institutions, a system as familiar with electrically charged barbed wire, murder, and dehumanization as the one symbolized by Auschwitz.

Are we dealing with a work of propaganda, a farce perhaps, in the last analysis with both? Peter Weiss chose to combine in the single figure of the prosecuting attorney all the district attorneys and the representatives of the secondary accusers. By this procedure, Kaul, the East German lawyer, a highly controversial figure, is made into the physical representative of the charge. The frantic attempt to place the blame for the existence of the ex- termination camps not upon Nazi Germany alone, but upon the capitalist system as a whole must therefore be understood as the intention of an author who sees a common denominator for fascism and capitalism. In the play counsel for the defense, also a composite figure, is inflated to the "Western World." His questions, to take the sting out of the witnesses' statements and cast doubt on their veracity, represent the mentality of an in- corrigible, stubborn society. While the judge and the prosecuting attorney stand for the principle of seeking out truth, defense counsel embodies the prevention of that principle. The trial dealing with Auschwitz inadvert- ently turns into scholastic debate. The question arises whether the proffered accumulation of data still reflects the total image, in which material and meaning achieve maximal identification or whether only certain features chosen by the author take shape onstage. Thus the ending can be considered as pure mockery.

The opposing lines are Kaul, the prosecution, East

Germany, the search for truth; and Counsel for the defense, the accused, West Germany, the prevention of truth.
Communists are pitted against capitalists, morality against
immorality, good against evil. Are matters really so
simple?

The information conveyed by this oratorio is certainly that Auschwitz was hell, a hell made by men for
men. But the quest for the explanation of this truth is not
touched upon; it is swallowed up by the cliché that the
phenomenon of an Auschwitz is the inevitable consequence
of capitalist exploitation. The connections between Auschwitz and the conglomerate of National Socialist ideology
is nowhere brought to light, the historical references are
lacking. An "objective" case history would certainly
have better served the cause of consciousness raising.

The Investigation is an early example of the limits
set for a play that aspires to be at the same time theater
of documentation, a work of art, and a proselytizing
sermon. It is impossible to combine the alienating form
of the oratorio—since alienation was presumably the
motive that determined the choice of form—with the
effort for documentation. This uneasy alliance results in
grotesque distortion, with an involuntary undertone of
parody which the reader or spectator ignores only out of
a feeling of awe.

Peter Weiss wrote his "Preliminary Exercise" in
1965. Is there a connection between the Auschwitz play
and the loose rhythms of the "Preliminary Exercise"?
In early 1965, in an interview, Weiss stated that he was
at work on his own version of the *Divine Comedy*, a
"Purgatorio, with jazz insertions and with dancing, in
the style of a musical." Weiss used almost the same words
in the "Preliminary Exercise." According to Weiss's basic
structure, the inferno harbors all the persons who continue to live with impunity, unhampered by others. Again
he speaks of the guilt of those who, remaining passive,
proved themselves weak. The purgatorio is the region of
doubt, of wavering and "eternal conflict," but it offers the

possibility of movement, thinking about change. Then
the writer sees the landscape of paradise: it is deserted,
empty. If we understand the author correctly, the dead,
the victims find their paradise in the posterity he gives
them, in their presentation on stage. The possibility of
"investigating" hell appears as the condition for evoking
the image of paradise. There is no doubt that Peter Weiss
is referring to the situation of the Auschwitz trial when he
speaks of "superior powers" and the "few." The logical
conclusion is that justice can come about only if society
is changed, if the "superior power" and the "few" exchange roles. His subsequent work is devoted to this
purpose—let us call it the class struggle.

The ways of life in hell, purgatorio, and paradise
correspond to three phases in Weiss's own development—
the first "containing the causes," the second "the suspicion
of an alternative," and the third "the consequences." The
modern Alighieri—as he calls himself—suffers from the
realization that he "betrayed" his Beatrice because "fear
of ties of any sort" made him turn away from her instead
of taking her along on his "flight." "What became of
Beatrice?" he wrote in "Discourse on Dante." "Perhaps
she was gassed." In the same work B asks what prompted
him not only to study the Divine Comedy, but also to
choose it as a model for a dramatic work. A replies that
he had been planning a "world theater" and that he had
been searching for a "model." The theater of the Renais-
sance had always had its "oppressors" and its "sufferers."
Dante's image of the world was the "image of a world
intact"; he was in search of the "meaningful" where today
only absurdity and inevitability exist. This passage un-
equivocally expresses the idea that change and working
for change cancel out guilt.

Eventually Peter Weiss discovers in historical materialism the image of a whole world, free of the danger
of decaying values, which made it possible for Dante to
judge and to condemn. His "world theater," following
the "structure of the Divine Comedy" finds its meaning

and rules in the philosophy of historical materialism. His "paradiso" is the world of the blessed still awaiting their liberation.

In this sense *The Investigation* is not only the evocation of Auschwitz, of the "inferno" in Dante's sense, but also of the "paradiso" as Peter Weiss sees it. A secular orientation forces the author to set his "paradiso" in our world. But should he place it in Coulmier's world, in a world where socialism has become reality, in theoretical rhetoric? The author is faced with a dilemma. His solution is to establish an identity between hell and paradise. Abolishing the infernal nature of the world leads to the birth of paradise.

Dante's metaphysical interpretation is renewed in the utopian expectations of dialectical materialism, which creates a new curative perspective. In other words, "inferno" is the place where the wicked rule and where we let them "continue to rule"; where the "mighty of this world" sit in "their fortresses"; finally, a place where we remember the victims, the "blessed" "still awaiting their liberation"—their "paradiso," created for them by the "new" men and the "new" society.

The creation of paradise by making people conscious of hell, and the changing of that hell, are the sum total and the moral of *The Investigation*.

At the Gates of Paradise:
Song of the Lusitanian Bogey

The division of the world into two power blocs—the
"socialist forces" and the "capitalist-conditioned structure" has by now become a fact for Peter Weiss. In 1965
he acknowledged that for him the "guidelines of socialism" contain "valid truths." In other words, the "socialist
forces" are held to be identical with the "truth." The
politico-ideological definition of the concept of truth becomes an indisputable Archimedean point of reference,
the dividing line which is the condition for the concept of
"world theater" and its ruling trait. *Gesang vom lusitanischen Popanz* (tr. *Song of the Lusitanian Bogey*),
written in 1966, neatly separates truth and untruth,
morality and immorality; it contrasts black and white
with lethal clarity.

Like *The Investigation*, this "play with music in two
acts," as the author called it, is divided into eleven
scenes.* The number three also recurs as the structural
principle, since the voices of the oppressors (Bogey,
Bishop, General, colonists), of the chorus (the Africans),
and of the single speaker (an African) are expressed
variously in rhythmic prose, free verse, and rhymed
couplets. The constant presence of the "Bogey," which
dominates the stage, constitutes the center and point of
reference of the scenic sketches.

---

* The translation into English is condensed into ten
scenes. See also below.

The play opens with a mocking and disparaging diatribe against the Bogey, the symbol of colonial paternalism. Roughly rhymed couplets create an atmosphere typical of puppet shows. The Bogey—whose mouth has stretched "into a big yawn"—replies smugly to the provocation. He invokes the Lord God and speaks of the divine "injunction," the "task." Man, he says, needs the direction of an authority which will save him from sinking down into self-interest and materialism. This antiquated point of view is no less familiar than are the arguments against it. Barbarism threatens the world, the Bogey notes in justification. A "jubilant and obedient crowd" shouts agreement with these sentiments. Preservation of values corresponds to exploitation.

A brief pantomime illustrates the subject matter— the relationship of master and servant, of exploiter and exploited. The Bogey, however, sees the reason for the uprising of the blacks in their "lack of maturity," which makes them vulnerable to efforts to incite them, with the purpose of destroying "our ideals." After the spectator has thus been faced with this hypocritical alibi, the actors declare: "The Vicar of God in this world / looks to Portugal with confidence. / The Holy Father / sends his salutations to Portugal / Followed with the blessings of their mothers / the youth of Portugal hurry / to the defense of the Overseas Provinces." The scene ends with the Bogey's reference to the "Civilizing mission" of the Christian-Western nation of Portugal.

The coarsening and simplification with which Weiss operates are embarrassing. The ideal of the Bogey's world is exploitation, supported both by the "Vicar of God in this world" and by the mothers whose sons are "hurrying" to Africa to protect the "Civilizing Mission" of Portugal. A way of thinking that relies on abstraction and generalization achieves a grotesquely comical effect. It provokes laughter, which is hardly in keeping with the author's didactic propagandistic effort. The scenes immediately following demonstrate the nature of this

"Civilizing mission" and the reaction of the native population. In Scene II an actor, in a devotional posture, declares that the mission springs from the principle of a Christian love of neighbor. A ballad recapitulates the landing of the Portuguese and the conquest of the country five hundred years ago; this is to justify the native attitude.

A lyrical duet in Scene III stresses the agony of humiliation. Thesis and antithesis follow one upon the other. In Scene IV "the performance of power is panto-mimed." The actors demonstrate the recruiting of forced labor. Scene V accuses the "workers who are white men" of lack of solidarity. It tells the story of Anna, who wants to take her fever-stricken child to the hospital but is forced to iron shorts for the white masters. When she speaks up, she is physically abused and thrown into a jail cell. This scene ends Act One.

Beginning with Scene VI, Act Two reveals the countermovement against colonial exploitation, oppres-sion, and dependence illustrated in the first act. It demon-strated the desire for equal rights, for a change of condi-tions. Petitions are answered by penal expeditions.

Scene VII* informs the audience it is good business to invest money in Angola; the scene details the exploita-tion of black labor by capital investment. Names are men-tioned; among them the "Krupp Enterprise." In Scene VIII the protest crystallizes into action, culminating in the demand that the land belong to those who work it, that the products be used by those who produce them. This leads to the uprising of March 15, 1961. The Chorus points out that the Western World, the partners of the Atlantic Pact, looked on, pleased and passive.

A contrasting effect to this world of humiliation and exploitation is offered in Scene IX by the visit of a

---

* In the published English-language version, these speeches are incorporated in Scene VI. From this point on the scene numbering is always one less in English.

foreign Minister of Justice. Of course he sees nothing but "islands of peace," "equality of rights," not a trace of "force" but "all forms of education." He cannot detect the least suggestion of "colonial force." Nor does he see that Africans from Mozambique are forced to leave their homes because they have been rented out to mines in South Africa, Rhodesia, and Katanga. Scene X reveals the identity between imperialism and capitalism. A foreign Bank Director pays an official visit to Lusitania. He grants additional loans in recognition of and exchange for the "humane sympathy" and "unusual sense of justice" which Portugal had shown when it left German assets untouched after "the last war." The final scene declares that in Lusitania "everything is getting steadily better" and that the circulation of the escudo is 131 percent guaranteed with gold and foreign exchange. But, in contrast, we are reminded of the lives of those who oppose the regime, who languish in Fort Peniche.

Suffering and capital investment, exploitation and profit—these are the poles between which the play moves. At the conclusion the menacing attitude turns to open anger. Everyone falls upon the Bogey, pulling at it until it topples. The fall of this symbol—which has application far beyond Portugal alone, as even the most innocent spectator has by now understood—is synonymous with the destruction of the infernal in the world.

The play, a series of sketches with a propagandistic and didactic purpose, makes use of a great variety of theatrical means. Documentary material is added to commentary, reportage in an epic ballad style is joined by the summarizing chorus, and fantasy supplements song and pantomime; there are obvious elements of cabaret as well as of puppet theater. The whole is put together in an associative framework, resulting in contrasts and parallel situations. It is colorful, fast-moving theater with an unmistakable tendency to the "total work of art."

This alleged theater of documentation, however, is in reality a "documentary ritual of consecration," although the term may seem contradictory; the play attempts to combine the document with revelation in a sacramental performance. The aim of the play, as clearly stated by Peter Weiss with reference to Portugal in his previously mentioned essay on documentary theater, is the presentation of "facts for examination." His purpose is the rational assessment of the events leading to the bloody uprising in the Portuguese colony of Angola in 1961. Thus entertainment is the least of his intentions. The basic situation is a kind of court procedure: the symbolic figure of the Bogey (a scarecrow, a figure of fear for children) functions as the accused, so that it can be scorned and condemned as an exploiter, murderer, and hypocrite. At this point one may ask if specifically directed political accusation and documentary information can really be combined with cabaret and puppet theater.

We are justified in examining the intended documentation in view of the goal set by documentary theater. The question of mannered overstaging of a historical context reduced to the format of a school primer is not pertinent. Since excellent documents dealing with Angola have meanwhile become available, however, it is relatively easy to compare a few points of the picture projected by Peter Weiss with the facts reflected in the documents. On the one hand we have the "Western World," "capital," "monopoly capitalism," the interests of national economies, economic exploitation, nationalism, chauvinism, bigotry, concentration-camp methods, imperialism, the absence of class solidarity, the Atlantic Pact, Beja (the German Federal Republic), and the like; and internationalism, class solidarity, the claim that the land belong to those who work it, the just struggle for independence, the cry of the subjugated, desperate African, on the other. There is no question as to the side taken by the informed contemporary. But what is destructive in this parallelism is the fact that natural solidarity with the second party is cleverly tied into total rejection of the first. It is here made implicit, as it were, since the play consists entirely of confrontation. This black-and-white scheme, here clearly imposed for the first time, dominates all of Weiss's subsequent work, including his most recent play to date, *Hölderlin*. He is now totally committed to the Marxist-Leninist view of history.

Since the play is intended to reveal a situation made obscure by the person concerned, the question arises whether such a simple division of the world is due to naïveté or is a denial of the very element that is supposed to characterize any documentary theater worthy of that name. Two aspects may serve to illustrate the whole. Their treatment by the author raises the thought that documentary theater as interpreted by Weiss ought perhaps to be understood as anti-documentary theater. The first aspect concerns the role of the "Western World" and the second "the church." If we are to believe Peter Weiss—having been enlightened by his documentary theater and supported by it in our own efforts to "search out the truth"—the young men of Portugal are "hurrying" to the overseas provinces, in accordance with the familiar nationalist cliché and accompanied by their mothers' "blessings," to die for the fatherland. The "Western World" looks on with deep satisfaction while the blacks are clubbed down in Angola. And as though this were not enough, there are no objections or protests; the Pope looks with confidence upon Portugal—he blesses her weapons.

Let it be said at once that this critical evaluation does not in any way intend to take the part of the colonial power of Portugal, with its medieval notions of order and subjugation. Nor are the following reflections intended to defend institutions whose rigidity is an anachronism in the twentieth century, such as colonialism. The sole point is the question of information and documentation, which is inseparably linked to the question of the possibility of documentary theater.

We must ask what is meant by the "Western World."

England, Sweden, Spain, all belong to the Western World; they are units in a collective concept. Are they the countries the author has in mind, or is he thinking of the United States? There is no doubt that Weiss's partition of the globe aims his barbs at this so-called representative of the Western World, which is content and refrains from comment. The facts, however, tell a different story. On April 20, 1961, the General Assembly of the United Nations passed a resolution by a 73–2 vote (Spain and South Africa casting the negatives), with 9 abstentions, asking Portugal "to consider urgently the introduction of measures and reforms in Angola for the purpose of the implementation to General Assembly resolution 1514 (XV)," the subject of which was the preparation of that country's independence. The United States was among those who voted in favor of the resolution. On March 15 the United States had also voted in the Security Council in favor of a UN investigation of the situation in Angola. The records reveal a meeting between Holden Roberto and John F. Kennedy, after which the former expressed his appreciation of the United States attitude concerning the Angolan conflict. In spite of Portuguese protests, in June the United States voted with the Soviet Union and the Afro-Asian members of the Security Council in favor of a resolution urging Portugal to abstain from further repressive measures in Angola. Further, the sale of arms to Portugal was stopped, and foreign aid to Portugal was reduced from $25 million to $3 million. As its reward, the United States had to listen to Salazar's claim that it was supporting "Communist subversion"—such practice being common to both sides. The fact that when a new Berlin crisis arose, the United States had to re-evaluate its position and the importance of its bases in the Azores belongs in a different context.

The author of *The Lusitanian Bogey* reduces the role of the church in Angola to a telegram of solidarity sent by the Pope—who is the alleged representative of the "Western World" in any case. However, the white

Angolans whom Peter Weiss sees represented by the
person of Salazar also included anti-Salazarists. (He
scarcely mentions the highly complex situation in the
Portuguese homeland, which must be clarified, or at
least mentioned, if the events in Angola are not to remain
inexplicable.) The church, too, although representing state
religion, played a part through its various representatives,
who did not in any way fit the Marxist mold. Protestant
seminaries in particular, and some Catholic ones as well,
participated in the intellectual preparation for the uprising to an extent that must not be underestimated. (Besides,
the original Gospels, if taken literally and without reference to the institution founded on them, contain enough
revolutionary fuel, even if not expressly stated.) Accord-
ingly, Salazar's revenge was directed at these groups.

The collage of facts selectively chosen according to
a preconceived idea, which in turn uses these facts as
proof for its validity, does not promote the trait of the
documentary that illuminates reality. Instead, it creates
subjectively credulous distortion.

Whether the pseudologic of Weiss's conclusions (such
as Portugal is oppressing Angola; Portugal is a member
of the Atlantic Pact; therefore the Atlantic Pact—and
with it all countries who are members of the Atlantic
Pact—is oppressing Angola) is coincidence or deliberate
must remain an open question. The simple multiplication
of incidents may equally be explained by the requirements of stagecraft, which require simplification and
stereotyping. In the case of Peter Weiss, however, the
result read as follows: "We women of Cabinda / are
standing before the prison / We carry clothing for our
husbands / You sirs Policemen / we want to see our
husbands / to bring their clothes." The Bogey replies,
"They won't need it any longer." It is a widely believed
story that the revolutionary Antonio Mariano, who took
a leading part in the uprising known as "Maria's War,"
was arrested (two of his compatriots had betrayed him
for a thousand escudos and a bicycle apiece) and jailed.

When his mother tried to bring him food a couple of days later, "she was told not to bother any more." Is it proper, simply to generalize this despicable incident, even if it was not an isolated instance, in what purports to be theater of documentation?

It has been our purpose to clarify two points. The first is that the method of the documentary theater must fail on principle when it attempts to capture and to put on the stage collective historical events, contemporary social entities, or socioeconomic attitudes for the purpose of discussion and reflection. Their magnitude does not allow an overall perspective and detachment. Documentary theater defeats itself whenever it abandons the ground of critical rationality, which includes liberalism and tolerance—that is, whenever it sacrifices its purpose of enlightening and clarifying to tendentiousness and propaganda. Marxism notoriously rejects objectivity precisely because it presupposes neutrality and an open mind. But as a result anyone holding an academic hypothesis is no longer in a position to create documentary theater. The Socratic function of documentary theater is based on the conviction that man disposes of critical faculties and is capable of "ethical" insights. Such a form of theater, which considers its contemporaries as responsible, is "progressive" in the best sense. An evaluation of the opposite position is superfluous; it amounts to a reduction of the critical faculties, to stereotyping, and ultimately to an antirational attitude which leads to the removal of the documentary element. In view of some of the events that have taken place in the twentieth century, such procedures are doubly ominous.

Encapsulating ideas in a total context changes factual analysis into a theological problem. The objectivity required by documentary theater, which owes its existence precisely to the struggle for objectivity, becomes a vice, while partisanship is exalted to the highest virtue, so that the division of the world into sheep and goats is complete. Understanding shrinks to political acumen, and its insights, embedded in a theological context, are prejudiced. Thus, analysis of a highly complex phenomenon—so complex that even a scholarly work can discuss it only with difficulty—is reduced to a static confrontation of two theocratically determined points of view. The contest is between two religious disciplines; the will to believe suppresses the will to find out, to demonstrate, and to revise. Dogmatic ideological rigidity prevails on both sides.

Declamations
about Incommensurables:
Discourse on Viet Nam

Documentary theater is a "theater of reportage," according to Peter Weiss. The purpose of his play with the epic title *Diskurs über die Vorgeschichte und den Verlauf des lang andauernden Befreiungskrieges in Viet Nam als Beispiel für die Notwendigkeit des bewaffneten Kampfes der Unterdrückten gegen ihre Unterdrücker sowie über die Versuche der Vereinigten Staaten von Amerika die Grundlagen der Revolution zu vernichten* (tr. *Discourse on the Progress of the Prolonged War of Liberation in Viet Nam and the Events Leading Up to It as Illustration of the Necessity for Armed Resistance Against Oppression and on the Attempts of the United States of America to Destroy the Foundations of the Revolution*), written in 1966–1968, is intended as a report on the historical background and the causes of the war in Vietnam. In this case the stage action is not divided into eleven "cantos" or separated simply by numbers; rather, each of the two acts is subdivided into eleven "phases." Peter Weiss has held fast to the number eleven, with its reference to Dante. A phase is defined as a developmental stage in the growth of persons or events. In this case the concept serves to define a segment of the armed conflict between the ruling class and the exploited; it corresponds to a stage in the class struggle that, according to historical materialism, determines the course of history. Thus the purpose of the play is to show Vietnamese history as a history of class struggles.

It is unnecessary to relate in detail the events treated in *Discourse on Viet Nam*—the word "discourse" more or less implying discussion and treatise—which span a period of 2500 years. Part One begins with Phase I, set in roughly 500 B.C. or B.O.E. (Before Our Era), as Weiss prefers to put it. Eventually the first written records of a Viet state indicate that the emperor Liu Fang of the Han dynasty recognizes it as an independent state under China and named Nam Viet by the Chinese. Eighty-five years later it is annexed by the Chinese. The play continues in the same vein. Construction, destruction, oppression, up-rising constitute a bloody rhythm which we know only too well from the history of other countries. The identity of the oppressors changes from Chinese to Mongols to Portuguese to Dutch to French, to Japanese.

Phase II, at the end of Part One, reenacts the occasion when the Democratic Republic of Viet Nam is established; President Ho Chi Minh proclaims Vietnamese independence in Hanoi. This is immediately followed by French efforts to regain control of the country. The Indo-chinese war has begun. The Phase ends with the first air landing of French troops in Dien Bien Phu.

Part Two finally fulfills the promise of the title; it describes the "Attempts of the United States of America to Destroy the Foundations of Revolution" and acts out in speech and pantomime the role of the United States, which little by little took over from the French. Clearly United States aid to France—to counter the "serious threat / to the free world"—is conditioned by "economic factors." The text includes such simple statements as "If we can no longer control / the prices of raw materials / our customary profit margins / will be untenable" and "Industry can reckon with new major contracts / before very long." Phases II and III indicate that Ngo Dinh Diem is the puppet of the American "imperialists," "warmongers," militarists," and "exploiters"—their traits visible in this perspective.

Phase V is concerned with the enumeration of murderous acts committed by Diem's troops, the establishment of concentration camps, and the departure of the French. In Phase VI Diem again rejects offers made by the DRV ((Democratic Republic of Viet Nam, as Peter Weiss calls it) to hold free elections. Instead, supported by the United States, he builds up his troops and engages in acts of terrorism. In December, 1958, "the people of South Viet Nam begin their armed conflict against the Diem government." Phase VII deals with courts-martial and the growing influence of the United States. The subsequent phases continue in the same vein. The chronology ends with the prediction that the assassination of Martin Luther King will lead to open rebellion in the ghettos of America's cities; the black population of the United States having begun its fight for freedom, a long hot summer lay ahead.*

The closing chorus informs us: "The voice of protest / against the havoc / he is causing / grows louder / The humbled / and distressed / have had enough / of their submission / Every day / shots ring out / in the ghettoes / of their cities / . . . We know / as long as they rule / with all the great power / of their wealth / nothing will change / What we have shown / is the beginning / The fight goes on." For the United States, the "mighty enemy," has taken the place of all the former oppressors; it is that nation's intention to destroy all forms of life in Vietnam.

Basically the play is a single long reportorial monologue. In spite of the fact that statements by such historical figures as John F. Kennedy, Dulles, and Senator Mansfield, combined with "projectors" and "loudspeakers," are dovetailed into the action, the work offers neither analysis nor dialogue. It is not the history of Vietnam

* This entire reference is omitted from the English-language edition.

that is presented on stage, but the history of a country as seen by the author, selected from the sum total of actions and events, interpreted, condensed, and staged.

Within the loose structure each actor again embodies a number of characters whose testimony and conduct are to bear witness to the course of history. Historical figures perform alongside anonymous representatives of groups; attitudes and special interests find expression in the speakers.

The author designates certain objects to identify certain roles, such as a helmet, a shield, or a weapon. He indicates historical groups by means of flags, emblems, dress, and the like. The crucial element, however, is the word. Its effectiveness is to be brought out fully through gestures and choreographic groupings. The musical background is directed to the same purpose. The documentary material is laid out as "documentary ritual."

Again the work strives to be a total work of art, in which—as was already apparent in the *Bogey*—the collaboration of image, sound, and movement endows the stage action with a symbolic character. The effect is reminiscent of the tradition of baroque theater, as well as the experiments of Kandinsky, Kokoschka, and Sorge. Or, in the final analysis, does the work represent an attempt at reviving cultural-mythological theater?

T. W. Adorno once wrote that anyone who portrays historical material has to choose between two principles, both equally unsuitable—psychology and infantilism. The reason that an "adequate play about Fascism" has not been written is not "the lack of talent," but the fact that talent withers in the face of the "inability to fulfill the writer's most urgent task." These words must come to mind at any attempt critically to examine *Discourse on Viet Nam*. Weiss's reduction of the situation to catchy slogans and his predictable narration allies the play with *Night with Guests*; neither the formal trappings nor the elevated style can conceal this kinship.

Peter Weiss completely refrains from discussing any

problems, from exploring them analytically or through debate. Instead, he copies out actual events, simplifying them for the sake of clarity and structure and thus manipulating the form of presentation. Detail follows upon detail, uninterrupted by reflection. It is like a passion play, where the author is guided by the assumption that no one questions the existence of the Holy Ghost or of certain saving truths and their consequences, as though these were matters of course. The title may be a preparation for a similar assumption, since it promises a treatise, the account of a given event. The absence of a level of commentary, where the material could be examined—a lack already apparent in *Song of the Lusitanian Bogey*— is probably due to the fact that (not unlike trade unions in a Communist state) commentary is considered superfluous from the perspective of historical materialism, since the "truth" speaks for itself and needs no commentary. This circumstance results in the impossibility of producing such plays in what Peter Weiss calls the Western World. Presenting the revolution "as a report of executions" as one reviewer cleverly noted, presupposes the spectator's identification with what is being "executed."

The play can be called a monumental historical spectacle, organically combining the media of loudspeaker and slide projectors with stage action to achieve the direct confrontation of oppressor and oppressed on a (seemingly) documentary basis. The guiding principle behind such oratorio-like declamation with distributed roles, the chorus speaking for the oppressed population, once again is an arrangement of (seemingly) authentic material with gestures of the *commedia dell'arte*. Even if the author believes that a montage of authentic elements must yield an equally authentic product, his play can only become a distorted image, not intended to analyze but at most to evoke communality in a mythic setting. Appealing to blind faith, such a work can tolerate criticism at most on the aesthetic level. The absolute unwillingness to produce objective, analytical documentary representation is made especially clear by the choice of gestures and language. While the French delegates move like "mandarins" and use an "operatic style of delivery," the speech pattern used to characterize the Americans is reminiscent of cheap poetry.

In the first part of the play, such words as "conquest," "campaign," and "attack" still prevail, while in the second part "aggression," "total destruction," "slaughter" are the expressions that stud the text. South Vietnamese who infiltrate North Vietnam are "spies," but North Vietnamese infiltrators are freedom fighters. This is the vocabulary of propaganda; its aim is to proselytize rather than inform, and it is repeated with embarrassing persistence. Insistence takes the place of argument. (North) Viet Nam has become a model, an ideal, to Weiss, who is committed to the necessity of change and the effectiveness of the revolution. The distant land is a symbol of justice, democracy, progress, and liberty. It stands for the negation of everything that clouded his childhood, youth, and early manhood.

The Ideal—A World Intact:
Notes on the Cultural Life of the Democratic Republic of Vietnam

That reality can be explained down to the last detail is one of the beliefs that shape Peter Weiss's concept of documentary theater. "Such a naïve and trusting outlook can hardly be shared by any contemporary aware of the extinction of the subject and the immensity, the inhumanity of the object." (Adorno) Weiss's reasoning is based on the realization that though we live in an age when every opinion can be propagated and all forms of protest voiced, we are nevertheless unable to gain sufficient insight into the prevailing conditions. This precisely constitutes the problem with which we are forced to live.

If truth takes its directions from reality, is vouched for by objectivity, and keeps pace with it, then the concept of truth seems indicated whenever authentic reality is covered by lies and propaganda. In such cases the unmasking of a factual reality leads to the revelation of truth. In this sense truth was identical with the reality that was finally allowed to be shown in Germany after 1945. It became a typical reality because it was founded on the experience of all the people. The consciousness of a common past and shared memories supported a common truth. In the foreword to his novel *Tauben im Gras* (tr. *Pigeons in the Grass*), for example, Wolfgang Koeppen was able to express the conviction that what he had written about the period "shortly after monetary reform" had universal application. His specific examples expressed a social reality that could be verified. "This is exactly what we lived through" was the reader's comment. Piscator's monumental extravaganza *Trotz Alledem!* (*In Spite of All That!*) aimed at a similar effect after World War I. Common remembrances endowed the symbol with reality and led to the shock of recognition. The typical event, the slice of life, became realized, and its recall required authenticity.

The shock of recognition cannot occur if the conditions for recognition and dialectics are absent. This circumstance may obtain, for example, for a generation that did not experience certain historical events or participated in them only peripherally. If the group is imbued with skepticism, anyone wishing to reach this particular generation must try twice as hard to find the appropriate means for attracting its attention. If the writer cannot count on collective experience or memories, then high artistic ability or strong ethical claims, supported by his personality— which sometimes to a degree takes the place of a shared world view—may help him gain a certain impact. He will at least be noticed. In other words, an author need not bother with art to the extent that he functions as the spokesman of a community or appears as the advocate or guardian of a cause. In that case his subject matter may be history that is the history of *his* community and problems that are the problems of *his* community; he uses a perspective and a point of view in which the others recognize themselves. A nerve is touched, whether by a ritualistic play or by (seemingly) documentary theater.

But what happens when the collective experience, derived from the event and its contemplation, is lacking? Bertolt Brecht's life supplies an answer to this question. His plays are performed in the West because they are "intellectual literature alive with corporeality and wickedness," as he himself once put it. His characters are imbued with lyricism and philosophy made tangible in a way that raises them above ideological limitation. Their existence is independent of their creator. One may reject

Brecht's beliefs and yet particularly admire *Mother Courage*. A greater, higher, more humane truth is at stake. The more one-dimensional and abstract a character, the more obviously it refers back to the author, the more obvious its puppet quality. The only exception occurs when the work of art—or what is considered art—takes over for the author as well as for the community. In the case of Peter Weiss, this means that the sacrifice of "artistic truth" must lead to his dependence on a particular community—to the necessity of a common "ideological truth," at the expense of readers who look to him to give them art rather than propaganda dispensed with an air of superior knowledge. This "collective truth" may well have been the aspect that most fascinated Weiss during his visit to the Democratic Republic of Vietnam from May 14 to June 21, 1968. "How can a people living through its third generation of war find the strength to resist an attack the totality of which far exceeds the destructions of World War II?" asks Peter Weiss. "What is it that enables this nation to maintain its production and its social unity in spite of the devastation of everything it has built up?" His book *Notizen zum kulturellen Leben der Demokratischen Republik Viet Nam* (*Notes on the Cultural Life of the Democratic Republic of Vietnam*) is intended to supply the answer and to explain to the reader why the "aggression of imperialist technocracy, of the rich world" against the small agrarian state that represents the poor world is bound to fail.

In sum, the reasons that, in Weiss's view, constitute the superiority of the small country are that it has found its "truth" and its "identity." These are in turn defined by untruth, by the "lie" of "imperialism," "imperialist aggression." The "new" men in the "new" society—born of a "metamorphosis," as Weiss untiringly points out— are superior to material power because they possess inner unity and unanimity, firmness and spiritual resistance built up in the course of decades, of centuries. The enemy who attacks them possesses nothing but his power, he is empty within, he has no future other than to let "his own madness grind him to shreds."

The goal Expressionism and Surrealism vainly tried to achieve seems to have become a reality: art and revolution are bracketed. Faith in the future replies to the enemy's nihilism. The North Vietnamese talk of reconstruction, not devastation. To them, books are "weapons," changing the reader, changing the world. The "significance" of art becomes "social, pedagogical, and ethical."

"Reconstruction," "progress," and the "certainty of victory" oppose the (lack of) culture of the "assassins," "the world of the American death culture, with its corruption, its decadence, its misery, and its prostitution." It is "junk literature," "brutalizing films," the "moral bankruptcy of modernism, which can oppose the outside world only with a subjective vision, with mockery and rejection, which turns to outsiders, or to an elite of specialists." The alternative is a theater for the people which is at the same time art.

Thus *Notes* deepens and complements the picture projected by *Discourse on Viet Nam*. Personal observations and conversations with the North Vietnamese show clearly why Weiss is attracted to this world. When, for example he notes that Nguyen Tuan, a writer, developed from "an individualist and aesthete" into a "revolutionary," the remark can be read as a direct, literal reference to *Leavetaking, Vanishing Point*, and the Marat invented by the author, who ultimately defeats the Sade who was also invented by the author. The emphasis on the "necessity to make a decision, to take a stand" recalls similar exhortations in *Vanishing Point*. The identification of the surrounding world with personal needs, with personal beliefs gained through soul-searching debates with the possibilities of the self, however, is likely to lead to the identification of the enemy with "stagnation" and "decay." The outcome is mythification, a consequence of the age-old yearning for identity of knowledge and belief, for unity and a compelling truth—for a world intact. Ultimately we are dealing with the confrontation of two spheres defined by pairs of opposites: nihilism and faith in the future; devastation and reconstruction; death culture, decadence, corruption and beauty, dignity; extravagance and poverty.

In the concluding section Weiss relates a conversation with the pilot of an American bomber shot down over North Vietnam. The major projects an image of "total alienation." He has never learned to be the "master of his own decisions." His tremor is seen as the "tremor of an emptiness in which there are only mechanical motions." His "entire existence" seems empty of "ideas"; he is a man who has never asked the way; he is a "murderer and a brute"—who pulls a murderer switch, ultimately like the murderers behind a desk of Nazi Germany. The parallels and the projection are unmistakable. "He is a component of a system that excludes questions . . . that does not acknowledge ideas." Equally unmistakable is the fact that the attributes which define his harshly seen existence—uprooted, passive, empty, bereft of ideas—also apply to certain situations described in *Leavetaking* and *Vanishing Point*, when the narrator felt no less a "prisoner," a tortured and humiliated being. The "feeling of abandonment" that caused these young Americans who were returning home from Vietnam "to weep" recalls another "feeling of desolation," another "abandonment," which has since been overcome.

When Weiss deplores the "blind selfishness of Europe," the "treason committed hourly and daily against this country," the reader clearly recognizes the scene in which the narrator of *Vanishing Point* accuses himself of passivity, flight, cowardice, and "nonparticipation" and asks, "But what shall I do?" The question has been answered.

Leavetaking is the title of Peter Weiss's first analytical autobiographical work. It ends with the image of the hunter in whom the hunted recognizes himself. The narrator finally frees himself from the "superior force" of the mother, of the family, and leaves "the fortress" called home. It is clear that *Discourse on Viet Nam* and *Notes* speak to a similar process; the subject is a country's effort to liberate itself, to sever its ties to a way of life that has been forced upon it, to free itself from the tutelage of a colonial master. Reduced to the simplest formula, it is the father-son conflict on a larger-than-individual scale. An entire nation takes the place of the individual.

The Revolution as a Creed:
Trotsky in Exile

Peter Weiss sees a "new humanism" in the literature of Vietnam (of the North and of the free part of the South); it manifests endurance, patience, and the solidity of forces undefeated by inhuman conditions. In his opinion, it is the "literature of the Last World, the one we call the third, and which will prove to be the Strongest." No proof is offered for this thesis. A turning toward Arcadian speculation, toward a new, third point of view, which hopes to overcome dualism by a changed utopian projection, finds its expression in Weiss's penultimate work to date, *Trotzki im Exil* (tr. *Trotsky in Exile*).

Trotsky and the Russian revolution furnish the theme of this play in two acts and fifteen scenes, written between November, 1968, and June, 1969. The propagator of the idea of the permanent revolution appears on stage as the conjurer as well as the person conjured up. A retrospective vision in the form of a staged interior monologue (Act One) and a series of epic sketches (Act Two) complement one another. The sporadic succession of scenes offers visual elements which fail to coalesce into a whole; the jigsaw puzzle does not allow a total picture to emerge. The author's shadow towers above it all, a puppeteer pulling his creature's strings. He proceeds according to whim—or according to his nonrational didactic intention.

Separate scenes, following in rapid and arbitrary succession, show Trotsky in various "phases" of his exile, as a writer and thinker, taking issue with the crucial

figures and forces of the revolution. The stage space,
furnished with a writing desk and a cot, remains the same
throughout, while the time levels change to reveal the
unity of experiencing consciousness. The principle controlling the sequence of scenes is clearly that of a free
association collage, intended as a picture of the preparation, realization, failure, and continuation of the idea of
the Russian Revolution as analyzed and interpreted by
Trotsky, the revolutionary and writer, the person who
triumphed and was calumnied, a man who is as entitled
as Marat to claim that he *is* the revolution. Once more
Peter Weiss has built his structure on documents. While
the appendix* lists the works on which the play is based,
Weiss fails to indicate which lines are quotations of
authentic remarks.

The leading character of *Trotsky in Exile* is not the
historical Trotsky but the figure created by the playwright Peter Weiss. The same question applies to such a
cartoon figure as pertains to the constructs of *Bogey* and
Discourse on Viet Nam. Abbreviation, stylization that ap-
proaches Sternheim on the linguistic level, reduction,
converting some sections of the material by transposition
into new contexts—to name only a few points—may not
pose any purely aesthetic problems, but as a method of
documentary presentation of facts it is inadequate. Life
is beyond the reach of construction, without finding its
alibi in art. The outcome is a "bogey" decked out in
clichés, with a visor that clatters open, through which the
author speaks in order to present *his* Trotsky.

Scene 1, entitled "The Banishment," is set in 1928.
It shows Trotsky before his deportation; Bukharin is in
charge of the actual departure. The Politburo is eager to
make the expulsion appear as a voluntary agreement. In
Scene 2 (1899) Trotsky is recalled in the Siberian penal
colony of Verkholensk, where he has been exiled under
the tsarist regime; he is seen reading, working, thinking,

* Omitted from English-language edition.

and discussing. The scene ends with Trotsky's escape. Scene 3, also a flashback, shows Trotsky in London in 1902. He visits Lenin and speaks with him. Again and again the argument centers on the role of the party. How can a dictatorship of the party be congruent with the dictatorship of the proletariat? Lenin believes that the bourgeois revolution must come first. Trotsky does not agree; he wants an immediate workers' revolution. Peter Weiss holds the same view in his commitment to the "Third World."

"Then came our differences," Trotsky states at the outset of Scene 4 (Brussels, 1903). The "Congress of 1903 in Brussels" is evoked. Trotsky now understands a great deal, including Lenin's statement that the result excuses "all ruthlessness." The discussion hinges on the possibility of reconciling dictatorship with the idea of a democratic republic. It is the problem of the avant-garde, already touched upon in the conversation between Marat and Sade; in this instance the participants leave it unresolved and pass on to other items on the agenda. Lenin and Trotsky have different opinions about the problem of leadership. The party splits into Mensheviks and Bolsheviks.

The scene shifts to St. Petersburg in Scene 5, "Nineteen Hundred and Five." We see the general strike, the simple plea that is answered with bullets. Trotsky calls for "armed rebellion," the use of force to combat force.

Scene 6 deals with Trotsky's second banishment. Set in Siberia in 1906, it recalls the events of 1903 and 1905, alternating with the setting of 1928. Trotsky first enunciates his famous theory, "The revolution is here to stay." In Scene 7 Trotsky has been living as an emigré for ten years. He is in Zurich in 1915. In a dialogue, he and Lenin draw up a balance sheet. A group of writers and artists enter, the founders of the Café Voltaire and the Dadaists: Emmy Hennings, Hugo Ball, Tristan Tzara, Marcel Janco, Richard Huelsenbeck—"pseudo-revolutionaries," as Lenin calls them. They can afford to destroy

"our cultural heritage." While they demolish, he wants
to preserve it for the people. A fusion of the two movements is impossible; resolving the conflicts of the avant-
garde in Dadaism by abandoning a fixed content is
opposed by the dream of a new type of art—art for the
people, dependent on the people's judgment. The "new
art" is the same art Weiss praised in *Notes*. All artistic
endeavors are seen as serving the war of liberation; art
is political, and the artist strives for total commitment.
Instead of the "contempt for humanity" of modern formal-
ism, this "bourgeois aberration," we are offered realism,
socialist realism, a positive, meaningful art—which, one
might add, is only a step away from ritual theater. The
problem of the relation of art to politics needs no further
elaboration here. It has been discussed earlier with reference to *Marat/Sade* in connection with Surrealism, the
failure of which was due to a considerable degree to the
irreconcilability of the two tenets.

Is it by chance that this scene, together with Scene 8
dealing with the "Twenty-fifth of October," marks the
middle of the play? The armed rising has broken out.
Lenin says that there are no better Bolsheviks than
Trotsky. In Scene 9 ("Twenty-Sixth of October") Lenin
suggests that his "quarrel" with Trotsky might now end.
Trotsky replies with the conciliatory counterquestion of
whether it had not been a "testing of strength" rather
than a quarrel. At any rate the collective that represents
and corresponds to the philosophy has been established.
Truth, too, has been enshrined. Anyone unwilling to
acknowledge this particular truth belongs in the "rubbish
bins of history," as Trotsky expresses it.

The revolution has been taken to its absurdist extreme; clinging to its truth with its rigid content *sub
specie aeternitatis*, it has lost the truth of the revolution.
The scene in which the "oppressed masses" assume power
ends with the charge against Citizen Trotsky for "preparing for an armed struggle against Soviet power." An
officer announces the verdict: deportation "from the terri-

tories of the Soviet Republic" in 1929. The speech alludes to Scene 1, which had shown Trotsky's 1928 "banishment."

The stage picture remains the same in Act Two. In Scene 10 ("Kronstadt"), set in 1929, Trotsky analyzes the Party Congress of 1921 with its internal conflicts and the Kronstadt uprising. The revolution has been perverted; it has failed. Stalin, the "epigone, is an epigone no longer." But Trotsky does not become confused: the workers' state still exists. The conditions for building socialism still remain. "Internationalism" and "world revolution" are the magic words which will surmount the obstacles that caused the revolution in Russia to fail. Again Trotsky emphasizes the need for "terror" and justifies it by pointing to the "terror of the capitalists; the enemy is vast," especially American "capital" that is taking over one continent after another.

Thus Scene 12 is entitled "World Revolution." It is 1935; Trotsky has fled to Grenoble. His life is in danger. He is afraid. Students from different countries come to visit and ask questions. Trotsky's answers reveal a similarity to Marat's abstract thinking, with its readiness to sacrifice people and more people to the preservation of the idea, to justify death and the Terror by the future good. It is the "brain" that is speaking, ignoring the "body." When a German student mentions the discrimination against Jews in the Soviet Union, Peter Weiss's Trotsky has no answer other than that it looks as if the arrested Jews are being punished for criticizing the party leadership. The only way of helping the Jews is, in his opinion, to fight harder to restore the International. But in the meantime hundreds of thousands of Jews in Germany are going around in fear for their lives, the German student points out, and he asks whether those "left behind" must accept their "fate," since the Nazis are obviously planning systematically to exterminate them. Trotsky's reply is the height of cynicism: in the great confrontation the Jews' fight for survival is of minor

significance. They are merely the victims of an internal
capitalist quarrel. Trotsky speaks of "tragedy" and inevitability; he takes refuge in talks and metaphysics. His
reply is that of the true believer. The receptive ear of
another true believer may perhaps hear it as less cynical.
But then, what of Auschwitz as experienced by the man
once destined for deportation? Must not a Trotsky who
speaks in this fashion appear guilty to this author? The
questions remain. The German student doubts that the
revolution has successfully spread to the hearts of men.
He even blames Trotsky and his accomplices for prevent-
ing the liberation of human consciousness. Trotsky "jumps
up angrily." He feebly points out that revolution is
possible only by means of "extreme violence." But the
student inquires further. Where is the new socialist man,
free of selfishness, ambition, competitive instincts, and
base designs? Trotsky's reply is monumental, flat, and
orthodox: for all its "deformities," the socialist state
represents the greatest advance that men have ever made.
Trotsky, murdered in 1940, lived long enough to see the
pact between Stalin and Hitler.

In Scene 13 Trotsky is shown as an "enemy of the
people," whose cohorts are sentenced during the show
trials (1936–1938). Trotsky has a vision in which he
participates in the trials where he is denounced as a
counterrevolutionary, an enemy of socialism. It becomes
clear that Trotsky—who can witness the drama but not
intervene in it—sees through the claims of the proletarian
advance guard. But instead of drawing from this fact
the conclusions that doom him to failure and show that
his work has been in vain, Peter Weiss's hero frees himself from the contradiction by replacing matters that call
for proof with something that has apparently been proved.
The demand for the "new man," which has been raised
since time immemorial, is buried under the exaltation of
the existing new man. The idea grips him more strongly
than does the bloody reality.

Peter Weiss's Trotsky reacts to the show trials with

blindness; he puts his trust in proofs he is eager to furnish. The definition of truth as "partisan," as "party truth," postulated by Lenin and others, is now directed against him. The accused Zinoviev conclusively sums up the situation. At the last reckoning the party is always right, because it is the only historical instrument the working classes have to fulfill their purposes. Nonetheless, Trotsky's blindness and his "materialist idealism" enable him to cling to the idea of the revolution.

Breton appears in Scene 14, which is set in the Mexican exile ("The Testament"). He asserts that victims as well as executioners allowed themselves to be made into scapegoats by the show trials—the former because of their eagerness to suffer, the latter because of their tyranny—both doing irreparable harm to the cause of socialism. Trotsky retorts that this is not proof that socialism is wrong, but of the weakness and inexperience directing revolutionary acts. While Breton sees the bankruptcy of the revolutionaries' ideas, Trotsky is satisfied with the thought that it is not the idea, but fallible man, that is at fault.

The intellectual error made by both the author and his protagonist consists in their concept—derived from Hegel —that the idea is both objective truth and true being. Since it is considered the primary principle, reality always has an alibi, in the tenets of dialectical materialism; conditioned solely by economic circumstances, the dream of paradise becomes realizable.

With his killer already at his back, Trotsky stresses the fact that failures and disappointments cannot stop him from seeing beyond the present defeat a rising of the oppressed everywhere. He is not expressing a utopian philosophy but the "sober prediction of dialectical materialism." It is a manifesto of faith, which Weiss calls his testament.

The metaphysical element inherent in this causal mechanistic view of life, with the expectation of man's happiness, should not be ignored. The present is defined as a "system of absolute baseness, absolute greed, absolute egotism. That system cannot change. It can only, by its very nature, become more predatory, more destructive." In other terms, it is the condition imposed by "world capitalism," by the "threats and lies of the bourgeois regime." The higher future, which must combat this reality, is called socialism; it can change "in spite of the crimes committed in its name," it can be "improved, can be given new life." Only "international revolution" can ultimately put an end to exploitation, violence, and war. Then at last will the lion lie down with the lamb. Man's hope for the Messiah will have been fulfilled. Although the killing of Trotsky with an ice axe was *murder*, Peter Weiss entitles Scene 15 "The Execution."

In his essay on Dante, Weiss notes that in the first part of the *Commedia* Dante sketched the limits of inescapability and futility. There was no room for hope of change. Once again for Peter Weiss the territory of "world capitalism" is the same as the Inferno. The horror of hell is its rigidity—the rigidity that prevails in his play *The Insurance Policy*. In Weiss's view the step from Inferno to Purgatorio is the step from paralysis to reason. It is the kind of reason, perhaps, that characterizes the dialogue between Marat and Sade. And what about the Paradiso? Its description is that of the oppressed and the tortured. They are the blessed who await their liberation. They have been presented to us in *The Investigation*, in *Song of the Lusitanian Bogey*, and in *Discourse on Viet Nam*. Who will redeem them? Who will lead them into the true paradise, which is still a part of hell but also its potential? To some, *Trotsky in Exile* may supply a (theological) answer to this question. Trotsky becomes the symbol, a messianic figure, the redeemer of all the oppressed and tortured.

From this play, too, a direct line leads back to Surrealism. After his expulsion from Russia, and having left Turkey, Trotsky requested asylum in France; the French government refused his petition. In response,

Surrealists issued a protest that was also an homage to Trotsky. They claimed that he had invented a "formula" continually to inject new meaning and a rational foundation into life and action. Socialism, they noted, could bring about a leap from the realm of oppression and necessity into the realm of freedom. It is worth noting that these sentiments were expressed in 1934. In Scene 14 Peter Weiss's Trotsky discusses the show trials with the Mexican painter Diego Rivera and with André Breton, the leading Surrealist poet. (Breton's suggestion, voiced in the years 1927–1932, that the artistic revolution of Surrealism be combined with Marxist ideology had proved unworkable.) They do not discuss art, as would have been more natural. That subject has been dealt with in Scene 7, in a confrontation with the Zurich Dadaists. Heulsenbeck had accused Trotsky and his associates of taking art much too seriously; he had questioned their continued belief in "great works." Weiss's Trotsky had replied that the future promised mass art, "classless art."

These platitudes sound embarrassing—as does so much else—coming from a man as highly educated and sensitive as Trotsky. More importantly, they conflict with Nadeau's description of Rivera's and Breton's visit to Trotsky in Mexico in 1938, which Peter Weiss has presumably worked into Scene 14. According to Nadeau, Breton had found Trotsky to have an open, understanding mind. In Trotsky's view art in 1938 must work solely according to its own concepts and must remain autonomous. The struggle for artistic truth, in the sense of an artist's unwavering allegiance to his inner self, seemed to Trotsky the only practical guideline. A letter from Trotsky to Breton notes that truly independent artistic creation is infallibly revolutionary by its very attitude, since it is no longer able to seek a way out of intolerable, oppressive social conditions. Though Trotsky wrote this letter under the pressure of political events, the events of 1939, and subsequently to the present day, give little reason to assume that he would have retreated from this opinion, which differs markedly from the views he expressed in *Literature and Revolution* (1924).

Why did Peter Weiss prefer to set up a confrontation between Dadaism and historical materialism rather than face the latter with the aesthetic aspects of Trotskyism? In the first case the contrast is certainly more effective. It can be seen as anarchistic nihilism versus a new aesthetic system. The Dadaist's program serves only as a colorless background, against which the positive new art stands out all the more luminously. Such a juxtaposition fits neatly into Weiss's plan. Trotsky's remarks on artistic creation reflect an entirely different opinion, however, according to Breton's account of one of their conversations. They express something like a "third point of view," since they grant autonomy to art, and such an attitude has no place in a world radically divided into good and evil. Peter Weiss's Trotsky is a "theologized" Trotsky, a legendary figure.

The written and verbal statements of the historical Trotsky indicate that he had no difficulty differentiating between reality and dream, knowledge and belief. If we accept him as a dreamer portrayed in *Trotsky in Exile*, the reader must of necessity gain the impression that the play of which he is the protagonist is the exact opposite of what the author supposedly intended—a play about the refutation of the "sober prediction of a dialectical materialist." It is precisely the fate of the great revolutionary and the further development of the Bolshevik party into a bourgeois bureaucracy that irrefutably proves that history does not follow a set of laws in the Marxist sense. In that sense man himself is the director of his historical drama—incorrigible, unchangeable because he is tied to his human existence. For Weiss's play this means that it must be viewed from a perspective similar to that of *Marat/Sade*—as a grotesque. Trotsky the phrasemonger is related to Coulmier, and reality is the Bolshevik fact. For the second time reality has caught up with literature.

Peter Weiss's tendentious, didactic play is borne on a hunger for wholeness. It paints an idealized Trotsky, who knew how to combine art and revolution within his life. His personality offers reconciliation to a world torn from within. It becomes the symbol in which documentation fuses with the pipe dream. Just as Weiss used to find his own desires and problems expressed by his favorite writers, "his" Trotsky "embodies" salvation, a meaningful philosophy of life that answers every question. Revolt against his parents, bourgeois society, and the Western World has resulted in submission to the discipline of an ideology that promises the fulfillment of his desire for a life that includes art and politics in equal measure. In *Die Idee der Staatsraison in der neueren Geschichte* (*The Idea of the Raison d'état in Contemporary History*), published in 1924, Friedrich Meinecke noted that the deep desire for the internal unity and harmony of all the rules and manifestations of life had remained a powerful preoccupation of the German mind, in spite of the defeat of 1918. We might amend this to read "because" rather than "in spite of," since the "superego" of the "Führer," with his "meaningful" orders, alleviated the absurdity of human existence for many people in a way similar to that of an ideology which unites all forces and demands passionate obedience.

The same wholeness characterizes the work of the writers in Vietnam, if we are to believe Peter Weiss's *Notes*. Its price is what the controversial Ernst Troeltsch has pertinently called the peculiar German tendency to a "mixture of mysticism and brutality."

Death and Resurrection:
Hölderlin

It seems regrettable that Peter Weiss did not dedicate his
most recent play to Thomas Mann. It would have been a
most appropriate gesture, since it was Mann who said that
all would be "well" with Germany and that the country
would find itself only when Karl Marx had read Friedrich
Hölderlin. And Weiss's play about Hölderlin is built
solely on the encounter of Karl Marx and Friedrich
Hölderlin. The author of *Capital* appears as the conclusion and realization of the beginnings made by the poet
who wrote *Der Tod des Empedokles* (tr. *The Death of
Empedocles*).

Weiss likes to make politicians and writers join voices
in seeming dialogue. *Hölderlin* offers a tentatively supportive exchange between Hölderlin and Marx. They do
not discuss; they seem to be on the same track. For the
first time Hölderlin—emotionally disturbed, withdrawn
from the world—hears an inner remembering voice. "A
blinding clarity," arousing feelings of renewal and
revelation, fills the lonely man's turret when the young
Marx expounds to him the two ways to achieve basic
changes—"analysis of the concrete historical situation"
and "the visionary shaping of the deepest personal experience." Combined in a "documentary vision," these
two methods lead to the epiphany of a world "intact,"
ruled by true equality and justice, as stated in the
prologue.

Marx complains that he has vainly searched Hölder-

lin's writings for a dramatic work dealing with an armed
uprising. Straining the concept of reality, Hölderlin replies that if people say that he has written on a subject,
they must surely be right; perhaps they are thinking
of Spartacus or of Babeuf, to whom he had felt close.
Though the causal connection is not particularly illuminating, it leads to the narrow ground on which Hölderlin
may set himself up as a soldier in the class struggle. He
hurries to his desk to search among his papers, while
Marx waits patiently. He digs up sheets of manuscripts,
which he wants to have "copied" at once. His comments
must sound cryptical to the uninitiated; at long last
something can be done, at last the doors are open. His
provocative announcement is not further explained. The
man who has spoken these words slumps down on the
couch in resignation. It may be that he doubts the words
Peter Weiss put in his mouth; perhaps their half-baked
naïveté tastes bitter to him?

The idea is left hanging in midair, conveying the
impression that Hölderlin had actually written a play
about Spartacus, marking its author as a follower of
agrarian communism on the model of Gracchus Babeuf.
Spartacus takes the place of Empedocles, the wise and
modest philosopher who, like Trotsky, sees through the
contradictions of the avant-garde and the dialectics of the
historical process that usually victimize those who human-
ize and relativize the revolution instead of destroying it
by the logical application of all that is considered to be
absolute.

And yet—if Weiss turns Hölderlin into the author
of a work on Spartacus he is not entirely unjustified. The
four words "and share the wealth" do actually occur in
Empedocles. To quote more precisely "Join hands again,
/ Pledge loyalty and share the wealth / Then O beloved,
share in deed and glory / Like faithful Dioscuri." Is this
the language to preserve revolutionary monuments? In
his vast, scholarly *Hölderlin und die französische Revolution* (*Hölderlin and the French Revolution*), in which

speculation outweighs new facts and which probably
served Peter Weiss as source material, Pierre Bertaux expresses the opinion that Hölderlin "even went a step further than Jacobinism, and a considerable step at that." The
four words lead him to suspect that in the spring of 1797
Hölderlin avidly followed the newspaper reports of
Gracchus Babeuf's Paris trials. A few months before
Hölderlin allegedly wrote the lines in question, Babeuf
had been condemned to death and executed. That is all—
a tiny flame which is meant to change night into broad
daylight. Weiss's vision gives us an image of Hölderlin
that is anchored in Hölderlin's actual life only by a few
selected citations, which have been incorporated in the
text without quotation marks. Thus the play that bears
his name is based on a combination of documents and
artistic vision.

The possibility—or rather, the questionability—of
such a procedure need not be examined again. The question is what relation there is between the Hölderlin of
Peter Weiss's play and the Hölderlin known to be the
author of *Hyperion*. To what extent do aesthetic correctness and factual correctness coincide, since the play does,
after all, bear the name of a German poet, makes use of
programmed association, and presents verifiable facts on
stage? This question can be answered most readily if we
take a position wholly unaffected by historical knowledge
to grasp the view Weiss's *Hölderlin* offers the reader or
spectator. An obvious view, for instance, is the angle
from which Montesquieu's Persian travelers Rica and
Urbek (*Persian Letters*) describe their impressions of
Europe in their letters. Let us assume that one of the two
innocents, unspoiled by the "brainwashing" of any
bourgeois ideology, were to read the play. How would it
appear to him?

In two acts of eight scenes with a prologue and epilogue, a "singer" presents scenes from the life of a
German poet. It begins with Hölderlin's early rebellion
against tyranny, followed by immediate punishment in

the form of a "public beating" given to one of his friends by Ephorus Schnurrer. In the second scene the hero sets out to earn his living, which gives him the opportunity to prove his (German) resolution in the von Kalb residence, where he is exposed to the liberal advances of Mrs. von Kalb's lady companion, "the Kirms woman," and to divert young Master Kalb from his debilitating vice with stories about class struggle and exploitation.

The third scene enacts Hölderlin's visit to Schiller. The young man demands "total upheaval" so that the "new man" promised by the Bible (and by others) can come into being. Blinded by (revolutionary) zeal, he does not notice that Goethe is also present, and therefore he shouts "out loud like a donkey A Hee, A Hee." Next, the same "Councilor von Goethe" calls in the police to deal with students who, demanding headed nails, are disrupting Fichte's lectures. The resolute Hölderlin is among those arrested.

At this point if not sooner Rica or Urbek will express surprise at the fuss Germans make over their famous fuddy-duddies and phrasemongers. The fifth scene, in which Hölderlin "repairs his new pupil, Henri," will surely stimulate a different trend of thought in the minds of the two travelers. For after Hegel's pitiful discussions of the "thingamabob" (the thing in itself), as it is called in the text, Susette Gontard, the lady of the house, confesses to the poetic tutor, "I hold you incessantly / inside of me, my darling."

In the household of Jakob Gontard—who is worth "five hundred thousand guilders"—the poet experiences not only love and mortification, but also out-and-out exploitation. Workers, maids, and butlers never miss an opportunity to demonstrate the measure to which they are being fleeced. The chorus comments that on the exchange the stocks keep climbing. Act 1 concludes with the chorus, using phraseology, summing up the situation: "O Lord and Business / we project, we produce / and we accumulate."

It is this situation that causes Hölderlin to fail, in
the sixth sense. He has in the meantime gone to stay
with his friend Isaak von Sinclair in Homburg. The disillusioned hero now tells himself that every word uttered
in the "hierarchies" of the bureaucrats is a lie, and he
asks himself what the workers in the workshops and the
stores can do about the situation. Hölderlin interprets
his *Empedocles* to a circle of friends—with the help of
Wagner the glazier, who asks supportive questions. He
explains that he must "go hungry / because you /
look on perplexed / belching and bloated / puzzled by
my efforts / to abolish the misery / all around us," while
loving Panthea appears in a vision to emphasize once
more the importance of the struggle of the oppressed
classes. The consequences of such rebellion on the part of
Empedocles-Hölderlin and of his shipwreck are bluntly
demonstrated in the seventh scene. Hölderlin "is no longer
accessible to rational communication"; he is the victim
of exploitation and the class struggle.

At this point the events shift into the realm of
dreams. Characters who have played a part in the life of
the broken man appear and speak to him. Pictures of the
imagination develop into a scene. The singer, a mixture
of minstrel and master of ceremonies, finally asks whether
Hölderlin's rejection of the revolution was only pretense
or mockery. This scene leads into the final one with an
unmistakable message. Hölderlin, in whom "lucidity has
been robbed of its force" by "unremitting pressure,"
awakens from his lethargy as Marx gives him the pass-
word. This is more or less the way the play must strike
the unprepared reader.

Peter Weiss's image differs from that of the historical
Hölderlin and the findings of Hölderlin scholarship in
ways indicative of the author's bias. A few examples may
suffice. On November 16, 1789, Hölderlin was imprisoned
for six hours for public misconduct in the streets. On
November 10 he had knocked a schoolteacher's hat off his
head because the teacher had once more failed to greet

him. Peter Weiss turns this historical fact into the political demonstration. Weiss depicts Ephorus Schnurrer, the director of the school, as a sadistic bully, a bloodhound, and the whipping which is one of Weiss's stocks in trade is here handed out by him personally to the students being disciplined, as a special delectation for the duchess. In fact he was known for his tolerance and liberal-mindedness. In the judgment of one contemporary, he "encourages freedom of thought as much as possible—that is, he does not prevent it." What Hölderlin wrote after a further meeting with Goethe—"The greatest delight of my life is to find so much humanity allied with so much greatness"—is hardly in keeping with the image of Goethe insinuated in the third scene. We need not even mention Hölderlin's concept of revolution; based on the idyllic notion of growth and maturing, it rejects violence and makes it clear that the historical Hölderlin was incapable of understanding the idea of revolution as bloody dialectical process. Such characters as Hegel and the ambiguous Fichte, who are made to expound the philosophical ideas prevalent at the time, are nothing more than reciters of sampler mottoes. Their primitive, narrow clichés limp along in "basic German," considerably below the level of Trotsky's phrasemongering.

Peter Weiss would surely counter any complaints about all these distortions with an allusion to the "social function of literature in the class struggle," and he might insist, with Lukács, on replacing the idea of "tendentiousness" with that of "commitment." For in this work commitment is to be given the value of (dialectically founded) objectivity. The results of Weiss's linking his work to the tenets of Marx, Engels, and Lenin is that it can be judged "objectively" only if the judge is partisan —that is, if he holds the faith in question.

Unlike *Marat/Sade*, *Hölderlin* is not dialectic theater. The dialogue has no heuristic function; it merely serves as a vehicle for a prefabricated philosophy of life. The initial dialogue, implied by the antithesis of Empedocles

and Hermocrates, both creations of Hölderlin, is not
played out. The author is solely interested in the confirmation of "truth." He assembles selected documentary facts
into a simultaneity of effects in order to achieve a
political propaganda effect. At the same time he attempts
to maintain aesthetic elements. Speaking of *Trotsky*,
Weiss noted that his montage and selection of material
was aimed at restoring "proper historical proportions."
What is "proper" is determined by the author—or by the
"party" to which he belongs. In this fashion his succession of pictures from the life of Hölderlin becomes a
chronicle demonstrating an ideological concept. Events
of Hölderlin's life, shown in the proper light, serve negatively to prove the positive value of a particular ideology.
The play thus becomes confessional fiction, self-expres-
sion toward a political end. By what criteria is this end to
be judged, since easily proven misstatements of verifiable
facts can at any time impart a negative connotation to it?
Though the appearance of reality through the use of
historical names preserves the mask, the hidden message
differs from the apparent one. Artistic correctness and
factual correctness are in a relationship of negative tension but they simulate congruence. A clear separation of
the two would at the very least have been an emphatic
invitation to judge the play simply as a work of art. However, as viewing the play from the perspective of
Montesquieu's characters has shown, once the historical
names and associations have been discounted, the play
is nothing but an embarrassingly rattling, involuntarily
comic set of cartoons. The tendency to the grotesque and
the crude superficiality are so clear that even the sickly
archaisms of the writing can scarcely cloak them with
compassion.

The play begins and ends with an allusion to the
"tower" where Hölderlin lived out his life and which the
author calls a "prison." Is it coincidental that the image
of the tower recalls Peter Weiss's first play, *The Tower*?
Pablo freed himself from his prison by directly over-

coming his alter ego. Hölderlin's liberation comes about in a different way—it is an act of faith. The "Marxist mystery play" has taken the place of the original "existentialist drama"—a transformation already apparent in *Trotsky*. Demonstration of the "essential" is intended to provide an "insight into the essential." From this angle, *Hölderlin* is a drama of martyrdom without tragedy or conflict, rather like *Trotsky in Exile*. Marx appears as the angel of the annunciation, bringing the joyful message of the Hölderlin-Christ resurrection to the "tower." He represents, not the quest for truth, but a celebration of the truth that has been found.

The process reflected in the total chronology of Peter Weiss's work, in which the antitheses strive toward resolution and reconciliation in a postrevolutionary utopia of solidarity and identity, is another celebration of its own end.

Afterword

This attempt to retrace the intellectual and literary development of Peter Weiss through an analysis of his work has brought out one central theme: the experience of hell. At the outset we cited Sartre's definition of hell as other people. They are the powerful. Their "natural" actions, their cruelty and inhumanity are a confirmation of their freedom, and this freedom requires dependent people, who are defenseless and weak. To experience dependence, lack of freedom, and injustice is also to experience cruelty. In his position as a dependent, isolated outsider, incapable of bringing about change, the victim may be able to regain a partial freedom by masochistically enjoying his suffering, thus collaborating in the performance of sadism. This view corresponds to Sartre's vision. This aspect reveals that, taking into account changes in time and social circumstances, there is a parallel between Brecht and Weiss's early works. Both see the human condition as determined by alienation, loneliness, and "infinite isolation." But while Brecht conceals a "tremendous will to live" behind his grim cynicism raised against chaos, a sadistic and masochistic obsession predominates in the case of Peter Weiss. Instead of anarchic revolt, Weiss celebrates autonomous pleasures, drawing the possibilities of freedom to the inward self. Comparing Weiss further to Beckett results in three answers to the "emptied" world preparing for its doom"

—Brecht's will to survive, Beckett's wish to "extinguish," and Weiss's "delight in the decline."

But such an attitude could only be a phase, a transitional period. The next step is accusation. In Brecht as well as Peter Weiss, accusation and cynical affirmation of chaotic conditions did, for a while, occur side by side. Commitment to the Marxist interpretation of history allows for a concrete accusation of society and its representatives. A perspective has been established for changing the human condition. But this is as far as Brecht and Weiss agree. Nothing in the works of the younger man corresponds to Brecht's appeal "to complete the completed truth . . . to alter the altered truth," recalling Lessing's concept of truth and diluting and humanizing history. After *Marat/Sade* Peter Weiss increasingly identifies with the static, sterile concept of a "valid truth." It furnishes him with an Archimedean lever by which he feels able to move hell.

Paradise as a negation of hell seems a realizable concept. At the same time Weiss learns how to represent it in a secularized world theater. But since lies and evil as such are dogmatically defined, are "controlled," and as tools of the "recommended" theater arsenal are considered as givens, the fluid interplay of dialogue must be replaced with a closed, rigid, single-voice reportage (in the form of a montage). The theater takes on illustrative, declarative functions. It does not respond to Brecht's urging "to think anew in every situation"; rather, it is a theater of ritual reenactment. The tension of the quest for truth has become a celebration of the truth that has been founded—in the form of documentary sacrament.

The aim of this study was to describe Weiss's road from his existentialist beginnings to Marxist world theater. It views the message of irrationalism from a radically liberal standpoint. Pointing out and correcting convenient oversimplifications, however, is in no way the same as speaking up for the fact or event that has been distorted or justifying whatever has been attacked. On the contrary. Since Peter Weiss shows no inclination to deny his preceptorial gesture, it seemed proper to take him at his word even where polemical harshness was unavoidable. In "Ten Working Points of an Author in the Divided World" Weiss wrote that it is "the task of a writer to keep on demonstrating the truth he defends, to keep on searching for the truth behind the distortions." No one will dispute his right to defend "his" truth. In the twentieth century, however, in an age of inhumanity, and after occurrences such as no previous generation has had to experience, we must ask whether it is still possible to speak of a "valid truth," as Peter Weiss does.

History has taught us that inhumanity always invokes a "valid truth" as its most iron-clad alibi. Moreover —man can change the world with bayonets and with science, but only art can renew it, in play, in illusion.

Glossary of Names

mentioned in the text
for which additional identification
may be necessary

Adorno, Theodor W. (1903–1969). German philosopher and essayist who had considerable influence in the fields of sociology and aesthetics.

Apollinaire, Guillaume (1880–1918). French poet, novelist, and critic, author of *Pont Mirabeau* and other influential volumes of poetry.

Aragon, Louis (1897–). French poet and novelist, known for his firm Marxist commitment.

Artaud, Antonin (1896–1948). French dramatist and essayist, theater director and actor, founder (1935) of the "theater of cruelty."

Ball, Hugo (1886–1927). German dramatist, novelist, and social critic, co-founder of Dadaism.

Breton, André (1896–1966). French poet and essayist, one of the earliest Surrealist writers, who published the first manifesto of Surrealism in 1924.

Clair, René (1898–). French film director, among whose notable films are *Grand Illusion* and *Rules of the Game*.

Curtius, Ernst Robert (1886–1956). German philosopher and culture critic. His book *Balzac* (1923) was a turning point in French criticism of that author.

Döblin, Alfred (1878–1957). German novelist, author of *Berlin Alexanderplatz* (1929), the first German novel to adapt the technique of simultaneity and inner monologue.

Durand, Jean (1882–1946). French film director, known for his film *Onésime Horloger* (1910), which influenced René Clair, and the two film series *Calino* and *Zigoto*.

Einstein, Carl (1885–1940). German novelist, essayist and

art critic. One of the most important theoreticians of narrative and statuary art of Expressionism.

Goll, Yvan (1891–1950). Alsatian poet, novelist, playwright, essayist, who wrote in French, German, and English. He prepared the way for the movement that became known as Surrealism.

Hartmann, Nicolai (1882–1950). German philosopher.

Hennings, Emmy (1888–1948). German-born poet and narrative writer, wife of Hugo Ball.

Huelsenbeck, Richard (1892–1974). German-born writer, physician, psychoanalyst (in New York), co-founder of Dadaism.

Jarry, Alfred (1873–1907). French humorist, dramatist and novelist. In identifying with the puppet king Ubu (from his *Ubu Roi*), he gradually took on in his personal life the piping, mechanical voice and gestures associated with his creation. The Surrealists recognized a predecessor in him.

Kandinsky, Wassily (1866–1944). Russian-born artist, active in Germany, one of the founders of pure abstract painting.

Kokoschka, Oskar (1886–   ). Austrian painter who developed an imaginative Expressionist style.

Lautréamont, Comte de (1846–1870). French poet whose work is considered the bridge between Romanticism and Surrealism.

Piscator, Erwin (1893–1966). German-born theater director, active in New York for many years.

Sorge, Reinhard Johannes (1892–1916). German dramatist and poet who introduced Expressionism to the German stage.

Spielhagen, Friedrich (1829–1911). German novelist, dramatist, and critic.

Sternheim, Carl (1881–1943). German critic, dramatist, and novelist. Some of his novels are typical of Expressionistic prose.

Troeltsch, Ernst (1865–1923). German theologian and philosopher, critic of historism.

Tzara, Tristan (1896–1963). French poet and essayist, born in Romania, co-founder of Dadaism.

Bibliography

WORKS BY PETER WEISS

(NOTE: All German titles are published by Suhrkamp Verlag, Frankfurt on the Main, except where stated otherwise.)

Från ö till ö (From Island to Island). Stockholm, 1947. Swedish-language poems.
De besegrade (The Vanquished). Stockholm, 1948. Swedish-language poems.
Dokument I (known under the title *Der Vogelfreie*). Stockholm, 1949. Swedish-language prose text.
Die Versicherung. 1952. Play in nineteen scenes.
Duellen. Stockholm, 1953. Swedish-language prose text. German translation under the title *Das Duell* by J. C. Görnchen with the author, 1972 (paperback).
Avantgardefilm. Stockholm, Whalström & Widstrand, 1956. Swedish-language essay.
Der Schatten des Körpers des Kutschers. 1960. Prose narrative. Translated as *The Shadow of the Coachman's Body* by E. B. Garside and Rosemarie Waldrop, 1969. Published in *Bodies and Shadows*, New York, Delacorte, 1971. Also under the same title by S. M. Cupitt. Published in *The Conversation of the Three Walkers and The Shadow of the Coachman's Body*, London, Calder and Boyars, Ltd., 1972.
Abschied von den Eltern. 1961. Novel. Translated as *Leavetaking* by E. B. Garside, Alastair Hamilton, and Christopher Levenson. Published in *Exile*, London,

Gesang vom lusitanischen Popanz. 1967. Play. Translated as
    Song of the Lusitanian Bogey by Lee Baxandall, 1970.
    Published in *Two Plays by Peter Weiss*, New York,
    Atheneum, 1970.
*Bericht über die Angriffe der US-Luftwaffe und -Marine
    gegen die demokratische Republik Viet Nam nach der
    Erklärung Präsident Johnson über die "begrenzte Bem-
    bardierung" am 31. März 1968.* Essay, written with
    Gunilla Palmstierna-Weiss. Frankfurt, Edition Voltaire,
    1968.
Rapporte. 1968. Collected essays.
*Viet Nam Diskurs über die Vorgeschichte und den Verlauf
    des lang andauernden Befreiungskrieges in Viet Nam als
    Beispiel für die Notwendigkeit des bewaffneten Kamp-
    fes der Unterdrückten gegen ihre Unterdrücker sowie
    über die Versuche der Vereinigten Staaten von Amerika
    die Grundlagen der Revolution zu vernichten.* 1967.
    Play. Translated as *Discourse on the Progress of the
    Prolonged War of Liberation in Viet Nam and the
    Events Leading Up to It as Illustration of the Necessity
    for Armed Resistance Against Oppression and on the
    Attempts of the United States of America to Destroy the
    Foundations of Revolution* by Geoffrey Skelton, 1970.
    Published in *Two Plays by Peter Weiss*, New York,
    Atheneum, 1970.
Dramen in zwei Bänden. 1968. Collected plays. (Volume I:
    *Der Turm, Die Versicherung, Nacht mit Gästen, Mockin-
    pott, Marat/Sade;* Volume II: *Die Ermittlung, Der
    Gesang vom Lusitanischen Popanz, Viet Nam Diskurs*).
*Das Material und die Modelle. Notizen zum dokumentarischen
    Theater.* 1968. Essay.
*Notizen zum kulturellen Leben der Demokratischen Republik
    Viet Nam.* 1968. Essay.
Trotzki im Exil. 1970. Play. Translated as *Trotsky in Exile*
    by Geoffrey Skelton, New York, Atheneum, 1972.
Rapporte 2. 1971. Collected essays.
Hölderlin. 1971. Play.

WORKS ABOUT PETER WEISS

Canaris, Volker, editor. *Über Peter Weiss*, 1970.
Durzak, Manfred. *Dürrenmatt-Frisch-Weiss*, Stuttgart, Reclam, 1972.
Hilton, Ian. *Peter Weiss*, London, Wolff, 1970.
Karnick, Manfred, in Gerhard Neumann, editor. *Dürrenmatt-Frisch-Weiss*, Munich, W. Fink, 1969.
Rischbieter, Henning. *Peter Weiss*, 1967.

Index

145

52